CW00706660

KIT'S
SHORT STORIES,
POEMS,
VERSE & WORSE

To Dave.

Many thanks for your support.

Tony Kit

KIT'S
SHORT STORIES,
POEMS,
VERSE & WORSE

ANTHONY KITCHEN

Published in 2015 by:

Stellar Books LLP
Dunham Gatehouse
Charcoal Road
Bowdon
Cheshire
WA14 4RY.

W: www.stellarbooks.co.uk
E: info@stellarbooks.co.uk
T: 0161 928 8273
Tw: @stellarbooksllp

ISBN: 978-1910275153

A copy of this book is available in the British Library.

Cover and content illustrations by Stephen Coppock from Vincent the Magic Bus
Studio.
W: vincentthemagicbus.co.uk

Typeset and designed by Stellar Books LLP.

Copyright © Anthony Kitchen 2015

The author has asserted his right under the Copyright, Designs and Patents Act
1988 to be identified as the author of this work.

All rights reserved. No part of this publication may be altered, reproduced, stored
in a retrieval system or transmitted in any form or by any means, electronic,
mechanical, photocopying, recording or otherwise, except as permitted by the UK
Copyright, Designs and Patents Act 1988 without the prior express permission of
the author.

For Kitty and Griff

CONTENTS

ADVANCEMENTS IN TECHNOLOGY

I've got a new computer
And I've learned to switch it on.
But I wish I'd mastered not even that,
'Cos I keep wondering where the day has gone.

I've googled, e-mailed and eBayed
Till my eyes go round like Catherine wheels.
With one finger pecking at the keyboard,
I know just how a budgie feels.

My life is now an open book.
Everything hung out to dry on twitter.
I wish I'd never bothered with it.
In fact, I'm starting to feel quite bitter.

It's only a question of time I feel
Before I key in something I had better not.
And then for ever and a day
I'm gonna feel a proper clot.

There should be a law against it.
Exposing ones innermost self on the net.
It's worse than confiding a secret to a woman.
And we know how widespread that can get.

On the bright side I've been to computer classes.
I've even learned to do a spreadsheet.
Unfortunately it doesn't help me much
With housework or changing a bed sheet.

Whilst at classes I must confess
Jobs at home I sort of shirk.
But I'm hoping to get a female classmate
To help me with the housework.

At e-mails, I have to keep 'em short.
Although I'm getting somewhat better.
It takes me that long to peck 'em out,
It would be quicker to send a letter.
So, someone to help at home it would be handy.
(And with a bit of luck some fun.)
And you never know if I'm really lucky,
There would be neither jobs nor computering done.

AMBER'S DAY

I'm in my rocker, nicely snoozing,
All full and dribbly from milky boozing.
I've been burped and bottied and had a little cry.
Now me and mum settle, for some shuteye.

Outside a motorbike burbles to a stop,
With a rattle and clatter and a little pop.
It'll be me granddad come for a natter and quack.
Oh! I hope he's brought Auntie Alex on the back.

I like Auntie Alex, and she loves me a lot,
She's bound to really, I'm the only niece she's got.
She picks me up and gives me a little love,
Pats and rubs, gentle as a dove.
Soon I'll be asleep on her shoulder cozy,
Eyes half closing, feeling dozy.

Granddad smiles at me and chats to mum.
Says, "Well are we having a brew now we've come?"
That'll keep him happy brewing tea.
Meanwhile, I think something's brewing with me.
That's it, with a grunt and a little push,
Nappies filled in a rush.
Auntie Alex's nose gives a wrinkle.
She says, "Mum, we've done more than a little tinkle."

Mum comes out with the changing mat.
I'm thinking, I hope Auntie Alex does it as she lays me flat.
Me granddad's all fingers and thumbs,
Not the best thing to be around little bums.

But in the past he's done his share
Of changing bums and showing care.
Back in the days, when for their sins
They used liners and Terries and pricky safety pins.

These days it's easier with disposables and Velcro.
Mum says that's the way to go.
Granddad says, the thing about Terries he liked,
Years later he was using 'em to clean his bike.
I wish they'd stop gabbing and have done,
And let Auntie Alex get on with changing me bum.
I'm lying here amongst all this fuss,
Inelegantly exposed to the populace.

Oh! Here we go, legs in the air,
Creamed hands wiping everywhere.
Now, nappy in place, job's going like a dream,
I'm all dabbed with powder and rubbed with cream.

I'm Velcroed up and nearly done.
Better than last time when Granddad come.
Last time he was without his glasses, the clown.
Only tried to put me nappy on upside down.

My aunts and uncles say he's going mutt and jeff.
What with his eyes and ears he's not got a lot left.

He means well, though I must confess
At nappy changing he's not the best.
Oh well, we're done now and it's bobies time.
I'm off for a little kip, so we may as well end this rhyme.

CHIPPY EXCURSION

The front door bangs, our two are home.
I sit with a cup of tea at the kitchen table.
I've got a muzzy head and my nose is running,
And at cooking tea I feel quite unable.

The pair of 'em barge in through the kitchen door.
Noses sniffing, no smell of cooking.
The usual, "How long for tea?"
Stilled on their lips, with faces quizzical looking.

I beat 'em to it afore they get all lippy,
And say, "Tonight I thought we'd have a chippy."
Eyes brighten up, that brings forth a grin.
I am forgiven the cardinal sin
Of not having the expected meal ready, so that they might
Assuage their work awakened appetite.

"I'll go, what is it, fish chips and mushy peas?"
"Oh yes, and some tartar sauce if you please."
I grab some money and the van keys.
Then off to "Seafarer" for three chippy teas.

Tonight the Giro system doesn't cause a fret,
I can go my usual quickest way yet.
Down Castle Hill, Bull Ring, then the chip shop,
And return by Co-op, Hayhurst, Castle Hill chop chop.

I drive by the brightly lit window, and give it a glance.
It's all hustle and bustle, straight in and out? No chance.
By 'eck, there's a fair queue on tonight,
There must be other home chefs not feeling quite right.

Park up, m-m-m-m, drifting on the night air smell that smell.
Fish, chips and batter, salt and vinegar as well.
The aroma fosters a heightened appetite creation,
And I hurry to get a place in the queue of anticipation.

Savouring the warm, tasty, chippy air, we patiently wait,
As orders are wrapped and served at a tempo great.
Now it's me, "Fish and chips three times and a large mushy peas,
And a sachet of tartar sauce if you please."

A stack of wrapping papers ready the work top upon,
Then a steaming fish in batter is placed there-on,
All covered over by a mountain of chips.
Already my mouth waters and I'm licking my lips.
"Salt and vinegar?" "Oh yes please, and don't forget my mushy peas.
And I've got a sachet of tartar sauce too,
One should be enough, I think that'll do."

Salt and vinegar on with a vigorous shake,
All wrapped in paper a tight parcel to make.
Then another sheet and another,
Then she does it again, it's no bother.
That happens three times, all done in a flash,
Whilst I root in my pocket for some cash.
All is then placed in a paper bag.
Now I have to pay that's the only snag.

Quickly off home now I've had my turn,
Through town and up Castle the rubber I burn.
Beeston Street, David Street, now I'm outside our door,
Van full of chippy smells, makes me hungrier the more.

Door's open already, I'm greeted by two smiling faces,
Knives and forks, and warm plates set in our places.
Bread and butter on a plate, and tea on the brew.
"Oh Dad, if you prefer, we've got a bottle of wine, just for you."

COLD COMFORT

This winter, everyone by now will have had a cold.
Fat and thin and young and old.
Babbies in push chairs all snotty and screaming,
Meithered mothers with headaches, eyes all streaming.

Workers on building sites, in fields, workshops or offices,
Waving around germy handkerchiefs while mopping nasal orifices.
Colleagues resentful, saying, "Shouldn't you be in bed?
Not spreading it around here looking half dead."

They keep away from the infected, dodging, repositioning.
Not thinking they'll get it anyway through the air conditioning.
There's conscientious bods, washing hands, flying about with anti-bac
Dettol and bleach and all sorts of germ killing tack.
Then there's them that think it's a jolly jape and a wheeze,
Making sure everyone gets it, with a thumping great sneeze.

Pity the presenters on radio and telly, talking all thick and muffled,
Which a lot of 'em do anyway most of the time, though they've not got
sniffles or snuffles
Especially the weather forecasters, but, we don't need to understand them,
Doesn't matter at all, if they're clogged up with phlegm.
They disguise their ignorance with silly grins, loads of waffle and chat.
And what we'll get is not what they say, it's just as simple as that.
They're very good at telling us about what weather we've had,
But we know that already, so, doesn't matter if their cold's bad.

Then we nip out at night for a break round the pub,
To find, we're stood next to a bod at the bar who keeps giving
his nose a rub.

You don't mind that so much, but find it hard to believe
He hasn't got a hankie, and is using his sleeve.
His nose is red like Rudolf the reindeer,
Could be his cold, though it may be the beer.
Ah well never mind, I'm bound to get one anyway.
All part of life's rich tapestry, as they say.
But I'm not going down without a fight and a battle,
I take that much cod liver oil and vit' D, when I walk I rattle.

So, where's that leave us now, what do you think?
Is it possible to be coldless all winter, and in the pink?
I think there's only one answer to keep in a healthy state,
Dig in, under the duvet, and hibernate.

FAMILY CONCERNS

Now is the age of fitness sports,
This much we have gathered.
As Dad jogs out sprightly every night,
And drips home somewhat lathered.

Hey up! Stand back! He's out the gate again,
In singlet pumps and shorts.
You'll hear him shortly up Castle Hill,
All wheezes puffs and snorts.

Our Mum goes Keep Fit whilst we're in school.
Looks great in a leotard.
She's looking slimmer every day.
Less like a lump of lard.
Mum's off tomorrow to dancing class.
Says she's getting thinner.
But tomorrow night she'll be that jiggered,
It'll be beans on toast for dinner.

Where's Dad now? He's at the gym!
He really is an ace,
'Spect he'll be pushing weights and bars
'Til he's purple in the face.

Feeling fit he'll leave the gym.
But ah! Now comes the rub.
He'll have strength left to crawl up th' Navvy.
But will he make Castle Private Club?

Dad looks a mess, he's all whacked out.
And Mum is pooped again.
They stagger to bed at half past eight,
Whilst we watch News at Ten.

We're really worried about our two,
The job's got past a snigger.
But one things sure, while they're in this state,
The family'll not get bigger.

OF DARKNESS AND DAWN
Prologue

The darkest hour is just before the dawn
When problems common sense outweigh.
During that hour we can feel somewhat forlorn,
But likely, things come down to size in the light of day.

OF DARKNESS AND DAWN

In the early hours of some winter morn
I was lying in bed, wishing I hadn't been born.
Eyes bunged up with matted tears,
Fruitlessly hoping my nose would clear.

Sinuses pressured, eyes veined in red,
Face reaching blast off velocity from my head.
Coughing, yosking, lungs turned inside out
Chucking up chewy green stuff; what's that all about?
I sank back on my pillows feeling rough,
God, of this chest thing I've had enough.

Then I started to darkly dwell,
On life and death and Heaven and Hell.

Several of my mates have already moved on.
How long before I would be gone?

Anyway, where will they stick me
After I'm boxed or fired?
When I've shuffled off this mortal coil
And finally retired.
Can't see any kin of mine
Finding time to attend to some little shrine.
And therefore, if not wishing to create a reliance.
I could donate myself to medical science.

I bet they'd be glad to get someone like me.
Not too big, not too small,
Easy to work on wherewithal.
Then I really started to wonder,
Was I making a God Almighty blunder?

Would they want me in the state I'm in?
Getting wobbly, nearly ready for the bin.
'Spose they would, though parts of me may be getting knackered,
I'm not completely useless and cream crackered.

So, continuing on with this story,
I thought I'd do some sort of inventory.
Knees are creaking, joints getting worn,
Hips definitely not as good as when I was born.
Hands arthritic, shoulder wonkey,
(Life spent working like a donkey.)
Don't know what they'll find in my brain?
As far as I know I think I'm sane.
Don't think there's owt like a tumour,
Though they might dig out a weird sense of humour.

Insides seem to be working like they should,
Which is a plus and very good.
Some bits will be useful, some they'll slat,
Or feed 'em to the mortuary cat.
Ears are iffy, eyes are so-so.
But hey! Whoa! Hang on, I'm still good to go!
What's with all this morbidity show?
Though I may be a bit worn and fraying at the edges,
There's no need yet to be making rash pledges.

And hey! Dawn's light is peeping through my curtain,
Bringing on one thing of which I'm certain.
Get up, get going, no time for tears,
I'm good yet for another thirty years.

'SNOT FUNNY

0 to 60 in a second to 100 mph....

It's getting to that time of year
When our speech tends to become unclear,
When with watery eyes and bunged up nose
We mutter and mumble jumbled prose.

Our voice sounds as if it's coming down a tunnel,
Our nose is running like a gunnel.
Head is pounding, can't stop sneezing,
Lungs are gurgling, coughing and wheezing.

People turn their backs, treat us like a pariah
Wish we'd be carted off in a black maria,
Taken away bunged into a cell
To suffer alone in our own little hell.

No-one loves an owner of a winter cold,
Think they should be home in bed, in blankets rolled
Unless it's us, who has the thick head,
'Cos it's not much fun home alone in bed,
We're up and out and spread it all about,
If I've got it, why should you lot be without?

PICNIC HAZARDS

Summer's here and with luck the sun.
So off to the park with the kids for some fun.
We've bats and balls and sticks for a wicket.
Ready to play rounders footy or cricket.

To Verdin Park we all are bound,
Where we'll spread our blanket on the ground,
Where we'll fill our beakers with squash or tea,
And balance our butties on our knee.

Where we'll eat our cakes and drink our fill,
And play our games till we feel quite ill.
We're at the spot, we've looked around.
We're about to put our blanket down.

The cry goes up, "Not here!", "Not there!"
Those doggie mounds are everywhere.
We seem marooned amongst a sea
Of doggie heaps, how can that be?
Methinks that I had had some notion
Scoops should be used for doggie motion.

At last we're settled. "My that's fine."
As Dad toasts Mum with a glass of wine.
The children are playing with bat and ball,
The world appears to be well with all.
We're up suddenly with a start,
A piercing scream has chilled our heart.
Our frightened eyes the grassy acres scan.
Oh no! Oh Lord! Oh dear! Oh man!
Victoria's nose to nose with a Doberman.

They'd make me smile, these image folk
With dangly leads and chains that choke,
With dogs that simply won't obey 'em,
That run amok, causing panic and mayhem,
That frighten the littlies and old ones too,
And pollute the grass with doggie poo.
They'd make me laugh, not shout or cuss
If not so irresponsibly dangerous.

So come on councillors don't prevaricate
Put up a notice by the gate,
"Dogs on a leash", and "No fouling" either,
Or else the owner will be in meither.

REQUESTED TREATS

Mam! Mam! Canna go trick or treatin' Mam?
An'na won't put any bangers in a tin can.
An'na promise this year I'll be a good lad,
An'na won't trick anybody bad.

Aw Mam! That was last year when 'e called The Law.
Anyway Mam, what's trick or treatin' for?
'E rubbished our getups, an' never give us a treat.
We didn't push his car far, on'y in the next street.

I know last year we thought it funny
To spread on people's door knobs honey.
Anyway, that's not as bad as some lads do,
Some lads use super glue.

C'mon Mam, I've got me cape an' me mask,
It's not such a massive ask.
James is goin' from next door.
Aw, c'mon Mam don't be such a bore.

Wha' d' yer mean, I al'us gets into meither with James.
Just because 'e called that fella names.
'E should 'ave bunged us a treat, like we said.
James didn't know it was a holy bandage on his head.

Anyway, them blokes don't seem to 'ave a sense of humour.
If y' 'ear of 'em smilin' it's prob'ly a rumour.

Anyway, we said we was sorry, an' apologised by letter.
An' said we 'oped 'is 'eadache was better.

It wasn't our fault Race Relations went over the top,
An' me Dad ended up down at the cop shop.
Anyway, James' cousin Abdullah wants to come with us again.
Said 'e 'adn't 'ad so much fun since Allah knows when.
Anyway, us kids do our bit for multiculture an' stuff.
It's on'y you old uns as go off in a huff.
Anyway! Can'na go Mam, can'na please?
I promise to save you all the chocolate toffees.

WAR GAMES
(1950's style)

I lived up country, in Norley, for half my life.
And I remember when I was nine or ten
The summer holidays that I enjoyed.
Things were a lot different then.

"I'm off down Woody's Mam,"
I'd yell through th' door, as I bolted down the path.
Woody's family lived on a small holding,
And down there was always good for a laugh.

"And keep away from that Hatchmere Lake,"
Mam'd shout after me.
But she knew that'd be the first place we'd head for,
Once we were out and free.

The Lake or Delamere Forest was our second home.
The places we loved the best.
And if we weren't messin' in water, or climbin' trees,
We'd be sussin' out orchards, market gardens and likely spots of interest.

'Cos come lunchtime we'd be miles from home,
Well, it certainly seemed miles to us.
Not worth going back just for dinner,
So, we'd visit the orchards we had sussed.

'Course, we weren't doing anything like scrumpin'.
We were soldiers behind enemy positions.
Or we were foraging with the last of the Mohicans,
Down to our last Smartie, sticky toffee, or similar provisions.

We'd scrawl through hawthorn hedges,
Which were really tank traps in disguise.
And snag ourselves on unseen barbed wire,
Curse the enemy market gardener, and soundly damn his eyes.

I remember one sunny afternoon, we were lying in a minefield, stuck,
Which doubled as rows of strawberry plants, wasn't that our good luck?
Then we heard an enemy tank start up, sounding just like a
Massey Fergusson tractor.
So we thought we'd beat a hasty retreat,
Before retribution became a major factor.

All good fun in those faraway days,
Risking just a farmer's and a father's anger.
But now we'd be lawyered, courted and fined,
With a record like a real head banger.

So, maybe kids today are just as well stuck at home.
Gazing at screens and not going out to roam.
'Cos what was then a spirited prank, now is a criminal action.
For we are run by bureaucrats, and a mercenary lawyered faction.
Retribution on the spot is now not allowed, though back then, the job
could soon be done and dusted.
But today 'cos lawyers own the sway,
The poor little soldier gets criminalised and busted.

SEE 'EM

See 'em early in the morning
Walking out the dog.
See 'em early in the morning
Doggy looking for a handy bog.

See 'em early in the morning
Sheepishly emerging from the park,
Doggies leaving little skidpans
For unwary children out for play or lark.

See 'em later in the daytime
Boldly striding around Moss Farm.
Tough Alsatians and ribby Great Danes,
Each one straining leash and arm.
Skinny whippets, curly poodles, panting Lab's
And short legged Scots.
Each owner turning their back, not owning,
Whilst doggie squats on chosen plots.

Pet now relieved, the owner is too,
And eager to be away.
Each anxious to leave behind the hazard
Left on the field of play.

So please dog owner bear in mind
Other folks' point of view,
We don't want our sports shoes, shorts, or children,
Stinking of your dog's POO.

HELLO SCROOGIO

I'm a bit of a Christmas Scrooge,
On Christmas I'm not really huge.
I put off thinking about it 'til mid-December,
Though the telly's been yelling it since early November.

I remember our lot full of motivations
Putting up loads of decorations.
From late November or early December
We had streamers and tinsel hanging in the air,
Getting caught up in our hair.
By Christmas Day I was getting fed up
Of continually picking up streamers and vacc'ing tinsel up.
And after the celebrations and jubilations,
And it came the day to put them all away,
No-one could be found to take 'em down,
'Cept muggings me the only one around.

But obviously it's impossible Christmas to miss,
Even if we persist in being remiss.
And continue to insist it's not around the bend,
And there's no need yet to get those cards to send,
And wrack our brains what presents to get,
As we trudge around the shops getting cold and wet.
Though these days now, there's always the net,
Which removes some of the stress and fret
Of coming home from the shops in the dark,
'Cos it took us ages to find somewhere to park,

And when we did, some peaked hatted little sod,
(Who thinks he's the council's answer to God),
When round the corner we had gone,
Stuck a blasted parking ticket our windscreen on.

That's just about our council's wicket,
We get hit with a parking ticket,
Dished out by fanatical wannabe cops,
Whilst we're just trying to spend in local shops.

Then, when we've sent all our cards, and presents got,
And we think we've just about covered the lot.
On the last day we get a card from someone we've missed,
'Cos we couldn't find last year's Christmas list.

On top of that we haven't received yet
Our lad's present ordered on the net.
Though we got an e-mail, which was a shock,
Saying, "Sorry this item is out of stock."
So he'll have disappointment written all over his face
When there's no iPad in his pillow case.
But, though he's no gadget to plonk on his lap,
He's still got last year's annual to unwrap.

The only time I'm on a winner,
Is after we've had Christmas dinner.
As I've bought it cooked it, and helped serve it up,
(And had a glass of wine, or two, to sup),
I can then have a doze and put my feet up,
Whilst someone else washes up.

But, no sooner have I had a couple of drinks,
Put my feet up and had forty winks.
It's time to start again and get some tea.
No peace for the wicked, as well as me.
No wonder I feel like number one mug.
And therefore say, "Christmas,------HUMBUG".

B.B.Q. JOYS

By 'eck! Hasn't it been good B.B.Q. weather?
Folk have being going at it hell for leather.
Having friends and neighbours round and relations.
I've gone mad and even bought some decorations.
The wife got all puffed out, and had palpitations
Buying buns and baps and B.B.Q. wings,
Chicken legs sausage and burger things,
Brown sauce, tomato sauce, relish and mustard,
It's got to be worth it, even getting this flustered.

Home from work to get the barbie going.
Only then, do you notice the lawn needs mowing.
Yell at the wife, "I thought you were going to cut it."
"Oh yeah! I've got nowt else to do haven't I? Oh shut it.
I've been buying buns and baps and B.B.Q. wings,
Chicken legs sausage and burger things,
Brown sauce, tomato sauce, relish and mustard,
I've got a right to be a little bit flustered."

"OK. OK. I'll mow the grass,
Don't get all stroppy and sassity sass.
Just lay the food out on the table.
I'll light the barbie soon as I'm able."

Right, barbie's going, will be glowing red in a bit.
I've even slung up Chinese lanterns and got 'em lit.
Beer's out, wine's out, napkins on the side,
We're nearly there, ready to ride.
Paper plates and glasses plastic,
Plastic utensils, job's fantastic.
Chef's hat on, pinny on, spatula in hand,
Raring to go, feeling grand.

Just a final glance to see if everything's fine.
Yeah, lager, beer and bottles of wine,
Buns and baps and B.B.Q. wings,
Chicken legs sausage and burger things,
Brown sauce, tomato sauce, relish and mustard.
Something's missing, I suddenly feel flustered.
Folk!! "The invites were on your list to do,"
"Mine? No I left that bit to you."

Ooohh so-o for breakfast it's buns and baps and B.B.Q. wings,
Chicken legs sausage and burger things,
Brown sauce, tomato sauce, relish and mustard.
It'll be OK. We can have 'em all with custard.

AUTUMNAL PRELUDE

The cloudy skies of early dawn
Are lightened by the coming morn.
Air is cool, grass is dewed.
When against a canopy of skies grey hued,
The wing-ed vees of geese are seen,
Flying back from whence, to where they've been.
Taking with them our summer days,
Our buzzy bees and carefree ways,
Our afternoons in beer gardens hazy,
Munching lunches, feeling lazy.
Under parasols from the hot sun shelter,
Feel cooling airs, no sweat nor swelter.
Soft breezes ripple canvas edges,
Sparrows twitter in the depth of hedges.
We sip cooling drinks from frosted glass,
Surprised how quick the time goes past.

But now, geese are honking, geese are flying,
It's early September, and summer's dying.
Late summer scents waft by our noses,
Damp leaves and grass and wilting roses.

But wait, we can have some good days yet,
As even further into the month we get.
And October doesn't have to be a bummer,
As we may yet get an Indian summer.
So geese, off you go and fly away,
But you won't take with you every sunny day.
Hope springs eternal from our breast
That the sun will shine, and we can rest
And enjoy ourselves with a day or two's hols.
And lunch again 'neath the parasols.

A CHRISTMAS PENNY

Christmas is coming and the geese are getting fat.
Please put a penny in the old man's hat.
What's that?
Penny in the hat?
Children writing letters to post up the flue
Hoping for pressies from Santa and his crew.
Eyes all agog and faces all aglow
Where's the money coming from? I don't know.
What's that?
Penny in the hat?
Don't you know we're in a recession?
Folk going round in the depth of depression.
Not got two pennies to rub together
Toes poking out and the sole a-flapping leather.
What's that?
Penny in the hat?
Off down town to see the banker man
And he'll lend us as much as he can.
That's how it used to work as we all know
Banks draggin' us in and lendin' us dough.
Greed feeds need regardless of the debt,
Now we look back with cause to regret.
What's that?
Penny in the hat?
Telly falsely elevates children's hopes,
Way past popguns and skipping ropes
To electronic gadgets with buttons and screens
To phones and iPods and games for teens.
A materialistic Christmas we now endure
Whether we can afford or can't 'cos we're poor.
What's that?
Penny in the hat?

Is it about time we rebelled just a touch?
Sayin', "Eh you lot, this is a bit too much.
We've had enough of spending money and plastic
To pay it back with bank rates elastic.
Let's get back to basics and look around
Keeping our feet on the ground.
Just a little bit of something to those who've nowt
May help us remember what it's all about."
"What's that?"
"Penny in the hat."

GLAMOROUS FORECASTING
Or *Storms a' Brewing*

Of weather people I've got a little ditty,
On why they stand there looking really pretty.
The idea's to distract us from the words and the maps,
With half of us looking at the women, and the other half the chaps.
So, we can't blame them, when, not attending, we're led into the folly
Of leaving the house without our brolly.

So they stand there, with padding, mascara, lipstick and curls,
And I'm not referring to just the girls,
Who, with bosoms and bottoms and smiley faces
Cover the map with rainy places.
All lips and legs they never seem to frown
Whilst they smilingly forecast it chucking it down.

Now in profile showing off their figure,
Now making sweeping gestures,
Trying to make things look bigger,
Now swivelling their hips attracting our attention,
Lifting our temperature in the opposite direction
From the centigrade degrees on the chart diving down,
Giving us grief and causing our frown.

All power to the elbow of these weather wenches,
Who try to lift our spirits from recurring drenches,
With body rotation, giving us a glimpse of cleavage,
As they point to what's happening in Felixstowe or Stevenage.
Leaving us fellers gawking and faces all aglow
Through News at Ten, waiting, for the next show.

Then it's upstairs to bed we're on our way,
Where the wife asks, what's she say about the weather for the next day?

We blink our eyes and try to think.
Er, I should remember, 'cos I've had no drink.
We struggle hard to recollect
Our exact impressions, as we reflect
On the forecasting vision we have just enjoyed,
And all the skill that has been employed.

Our knees go weak and we go in a daze,
As with a silly grin our eyes all glaze.
"Come on, tell me. What's she say?
Is it going to be a good washing day?"

"Right! O.K. don't have a fit,
As she pointed to the maps with her stick,
I can remember every bit.
I can see it now. I'm not thick.

Devon and Cornwall, and the Isle of Wight too,
Have a nice trim foot in a size six shoe.

London and Oxford and down that half,
A well-shaped leg, and a nicely turned calf.
Round Hereford and the river Wye
The thigh is rated right sky high.
The Midlands they were mainly fine,
With undulations and depressions absolutely sublime.
Further north, the pressure rises.
In mountainous areas look out for surprises.
North again around Carlisle
There's a one hundred percent chance of a smile,
And in areas around the Isle of Skye
I detected a twinkle in the eye."

Glancing down at the wife in bed,
No twinkle there, as she cuts me dead.
I thought these glamcasts lifted depression and gloom.
So how is it I'm sleeping in the spare room?

BURGLE TIME

(And the Living Is Easy)

Now money's getting really tight
I think I'd like to mention,
A scheme that I've come up with
To supplement my pension.

I'm going back to college.
In fact, I'm signing up to burglar school.
To learn to break and enter proper,
Seems to me real cool.

I've already got my stripey jumper,
Mask and woolly hat,
A big bag with "swag", written all across it.
And a scouse accent, I've got off pat.

I've got to change my sleeping pattern
And stay in bed 'till dinner time.
So I'm as lively as a cricket
When I set off to do my crime.

The course starts off with loads of theory
On how to con the social right.
'Cos we can't mess about working in the day,
When we've got this proper job at night.

Health and safety is fully covered.
We learn to lift safes and tellys without hurt.
Though they're not too keen on ear protectors,
We need to know when plod's on the alert.

Mind you plod is very thoughtful,
They consider us a lot.
'Cos with flashing lights and sirens,
We're gone 'fore they're at the spot.

Practical class is at pub closing time.
Though it's best if we've not been in our cups.
It's most embarrassing, creeping about someone's house,
With a sudden bout of hiccups.

I'm really excited about the practical bit,
Creeping about in the dark
Climbing walls and fences,
The whole thing seems quite a lark.

Now, job description and risk factor
Are more acceptable than they used to be.
What with E.U. law and human right
The victim's the baddy, not me.

If the owner finds me in his house
Their self-control will be severely tested.
'Cos if he lays but one finger on me,
For G.B.H. I'll have him arrested.
And a judge last year said, it took real courage
To burgle someone else's dwelling.
And no jail either for you, it won't do any good.
Boy! I'll buy everything that feller's selling.

So, there we go, I can't wait to graduate,
The law is on our side.
So whilst things are going well for us,
Let's rob on Tommy, time for us to ride.

ARE WE BEING WELL SERVED?

In line with current legal shenanigans,
We need to enquire more into the murky past.
So lawyers will have something to do,
Something really useful at last.

There are some really important happenings
On which they can use their crystal ball.
Events crucial to our children's future,
And indeed, of vital significance to all.

So stuff it all about gay marriage,
Or who on earth said plebs, or Cleggy's Lords reform.
Let's concentrate on things that really matter
And make lawyers earn their corn.

There's the intriguing mystery of Jack and Jill.
Did Jack fall or was there something about it funny?
Did Jill just pretend to tumble down after?
And was she trying for the insurance money?
Why rush him off to bed,
And cover his wounds with vinegar and brown paper?
The whole thing seems a bit dubious to me,
A proper dodgy caper.

And what about Humpty Dumpty?
Was it his fault he went all splat?
An oversize egg, wobbling on top of a wall
With no harness and no hard hat.
And typical of this country,
When politicians have clangered and made a tits,
They wipe their hands of it, and shut their eyes,
And send in the army to pick up the bits.

Then there's Incy Wincy spider
Climbing up a spout.
Who was responsible for checking the weather
So he wouldn't get washed out?
And what were health and safety thinking?
After the first downpour of rain.
The poor little beggar nearly drowned,
And they let him do it all again.
And where were social services
On that fateful day?
When poor Miss Muffet, sat on an unprotected tuffet,
And the spider spilt her curds and whey.

And as for Ba-Ba Black Sheep,
But best we don't go there.
'Cos the money that's wasted on politically correct
Is enough to drive us all spare.

The full force of government and judiciary
Needs bringing to bear on these questions immense,
In order to throw light on these serious matters,
And of really of important things make sense.

WHAT A GAME
(Rugby For Beginners)

Rugby is a gradely game, a proper manly pursuit.
It's played with a ball, that's not a round ball at all,
And has a bounce that's erratic to boot.

The game starts in gentlemanly mode
By kicking the ball to the opposition.
Then to make life hard work, you try to get it back,
With concealed violence, and controlled aggression.

Early on in the game, the ball may go into "touch".
Then the referee a "line out" will call.
This is when, two lines of large fellers have a barn dance together.
Then, chucked at 'em of course is the ball.

Once possession of the ball is gained by one side,
To the opposition posts they dash with intent.
To progress forwards, they pass the ball backwards,
Which of course, makes perfectly good sense.

Eventually, things come to a halt with a tackle,
Which means some bod gets thrown to the deck in the muck.
Then loads of guys pile on top of the poor beggar,
I believe this is what's called a "ruck".

By now, no-one's a clue where the damn ball has gone.
And the ref's even hopefully searching the crowd.
But when he thinks they've had enough fun in the "ruck",
He'll decide that a "scrum" is allowed.
This is the point where the game loses the plot.
At least, where it's a bit of a hoot.

In the "scrum" we've got "props" both "loose head" and "tight head",
And a "hooker" WHEY HEY, to boot.
We've got "locks" and "flankers" and a "back row" too,
As well as a "scrum half" on the side,
Whilst everyone else spreads themselves round about,
Just going along for the ride.

The three forwards bind together, their arms around each other.
The "props" on either side the "hooker" WHEY HEY, have got.
Then, glaring and snarling, the two lines face to face,
And breathe fire and brimstone and snot.

The two lots of antagonists waddle up t' th' ref's mark.
Just like egg bound ducks in a farmyard.
The ref calls, "Crouch", and the combatants obey.
Like tanks into battle, but twice as hard.

The two "locks" lock either side of the "props" bum.
The "flankers" either side of them,
Now number eight, who usually arrives a bit late,
Bustles up, to join the back row by his sen.

We've already had "crouch" so the next call is "touch",
Then "pause" then finally "engage".
Then the whole blasted bunch, meets with a bone jarring crunch.
And it's push and it's shove with a rage.
The "scrum half" bungs the ball in th' tunnel,
Technique exact to governing body rules.
And "hookers" WHEY HEY, hook for the ball with their feet,
Whilst everyone pushes and shoves till spit drools.
Bodies heat with the effort, and steam billows up.
Soon, poor ref's peering into a fog.
And with thrutchin' and pushin' and stampin' and maulin'.
The pitch is fair churned to a bog.

The "scrum half" hovers around the rear of the pack,
Ready to gather the ball.
Which is just as well, 'cos everyone's getting fed up,
With hands and faces being where they shouldn't be at all.

The ball's out, "scrum half", gathers it up,
And looks to pass it to one of his men.
Now here's the rub, according to the rules,
To go forwards we pass it backwards again.

So, forwards we go in a backwards direction,
It's a wonder we get there at all.
And with blokes flinging themselves round all over the place,
We're never sure who's got the ball.

It soon becomes clear who claims ownership of the thing,
'Cos they make a dash for the goal line suicidal.
But he rarely gets there, 'cos he's soon buried alive,
'Neath a wave of "flankers" and "hookers" WHEY HEY that's right tidal.

So, back the ref goes to try to spot this bag of wind,
When all he can see is everyone's bum.
So in no time at all, he gets proper cheesed off.
And therefore we return to a "scrum".

It seems to me rugger's a lot like life.
'Cos as a species we're certainly perverse.
For, when life's going well, and things are O.K.
We'll find a way, to shift into reverse.

But good old rugby's a decent game,
Won't put up with any of that soccer messin'.
The ref's in charge, no-one argues with him.
A good example to youngsters, what a blessing.

No play acting on the field of action,
No racism either we think.
Heat on the field is dissipated after,
With a slap on the back and a drink.
But you can see from this, rugger's quite a hard game.
Not for the timid or wary.
But they're all decent lads, who, if you don't like their sport
Wouldn't even consider calling you a fairy.

THE CALL OF STICK AND TURF

C'mon girls it's Sat'day afternoon.
Time to play some hackey.
Did I say hackey? Or should it be whackey?
'Cos hockey is mostly either whackey or hackey,
So where hockey fits in I don't really see,
Though it still seems jolly good fun to me.

The game can be played by either chaps or chapesses.
The chaps in shorts, and the girls in very short dresses.
So, us lads watch the girls, its excitement never fails,
Viewing long legs, short skirts, bobbed hair and pony tails.

The game commences with two opposing teams.
Each with eleven players and five subs.
Each participant has a huge curved stick
Which, it's against the rules to use as a club.

Mostly the rules are a lot like football,
'Cept the ball is played with a stick instead of feet.
And swallow dives are not rewarded with a penalty,
No matter how classy looking or neat.

Heading the ball is not recommended,
Whether in attack or in defence.
The damn thing's hard and travelling at speed,
And won't knock into you any more sense.

There's an interesting departure from footballing rules,
Where it's worded, a field player may have the privileges of a goalie,
And may play as a field player, but without any headgear,
Though must wear it when defending penalties solely.

This appears to me to be a little foolhardy at least.
Have you seen how hard them girls whack that ball?
I wouldn't stand in front of 'em in a suit of armour,
And with no padding I wouldn't feel privileged at all.

Just imagine it, defending that goalmouth,
No body protection worn.
I'd feel a bit like an army deserter,
About to be shot at dawn.

When the game is stopped, but no infringement takes place,
It's restarted by a thing called "a bully".
I remember them fellas from the playground at school.
But what they're doing in hockey I don't grasp fully.

Anyway, two players face up, their sticks touching the ground.
And between the sticks is placed the ball.
Then they whack each other's sticks before trying to clobber the thing,
In a shower of shin skin, blood, turf and all.

Now, there's penalty corners and penalty strokes,
And a thing called a free hit.
Penalty corners look quite dangerous,
I think that's the point at which I'd quit.

From the corner mark, the ball is whacked in the circle,
Where there's a scramble and a general melee.
Shins are hacked, and the ball is whacked
Makes good viewing on the telly.

Things happen so fast, half the time I can't follow the ref's call.
Or how he manages to see who clobbers whom,
Let alone have his eye on the ball.

(Continued over…)

But the players seem to enjoy the game,
And everyone else is having fun
Although it's a bit like "Gun Fight at the OK Corral".
Only between 'em they've got just one gun.
This game is not for wilting pansies,
Or them that can't stand a bit of pain.
If you want to know just ask our Abbi.
As she's now back, playing the game again.

SEASON'S END
(Or *Dark Clouds Gathering*)

Now the Premiership season's at an end,
Our teams won't be driving us round the bend,
By not scoring goals when they should,
Nor by missing sitters and raising our blood
Pressure right sky high, by missing pens, God knows why,
Which were awarded for them falling on their faces
Through tripping over defenders' bootlaces.
Or by imagining an elbow thrust in their mush,
Or acting like they've received an illegal push,
Which sends them clattering to the ground,
Then peeping through fingers and peeking around,
Looking to see if the ref's reacting
To their Oscar winning dives and overacting.
Then jumping up, no sign of pain,
When they see that there's no chance of gain.
By God these lads couldn't try harder
If they'd received tuition or studied at R.A.D.A.

So that's it now until next season,
When once again we start to lose our reason.
When we live in hope for the first few games.
'Till we cotton on the team sheet's the same old names.
But still we trust our lads will work some wonders
And not come forth with the same old blunders,
That the manager'll come up with a brilliant game plan
That will bamboozle defenders to a man.
But no, they'll still be doing the same old thing,
Belting off down the wing,
Then hemmed in the corner like a stag at bay
With loads of defenders in the way,

They might manage to get in a cross,
But if they do it'll be a dead loss,
There'll be no-one there the cross to hit,
They haven't got up there yet 'cos they're not match fit.

In their head they're still on their hols,
Sand between their toes and ogling bikinied dolls,
Sunglasses on, Pimms in hand,
Fancying themselves, my aren't I grand?

But the sands of time may be running out fast.
Money's short the job can't last.
Paying millions for players with cash they've not got,
Seems to me some have lost the plot.

And paying 'em tens of thousands a week
The economics of that are a bit of a cheek.
When lads who watch 'em, scrat for a pint and pie,
I think that it's one in the eye
For those who support 'em week in and out.
Buy shirts and scarves and give a shout
For the team they've followed from a young lad.
I think they'd all be a little bit glad
If players had reduced remuneration,
More in line with the rest of the nation.
Clubs may then offer a cheaper seat
More affordable to the man in the street.

'Cos as sure as eggs, the way they're going
They're bound to reap what they're sowing,
And all end up in a mess,
Just like the Euro zone, I think that's a fair guess.

OLYMPIC CHAUVINISTIC TWISTS (2012)

I've watched a lot of Olympics.
Games and events I've enjoyed by the minute.
And so much women's sport I've watched,
I got to thinking there were no men in it.

I watched the women's footie
By gum it's fast and furious.
And I just wondered, do they F and blind
And holler out phrases spurious?
I don't see how they could,
They're too busy, heading, kicking, dribbling,
They enjoy the game that much
They've no time for silly quibbling.
Although on some of the finer skills
They may lag behind the men just a little bit.
There's one accomplishment that they've got,
By 'eck them gals can spit.

I also loved the hockey,
The girls know every trick,
It's magical how they control that ball
Wi' nowt but a fancy walking stick.
They get clattered on shins and ankles,
Good grief them girls are tough.
But you don't see them rolling around on the ground,
Or crying that they've had enough.

I don't know which game I enjoy the most,
My bets I'll have to hedge.
But when it comes down to the nitty gritty,
I think the hockey skirts may have the edge.

The rowing girls have my respect
'Cos it's a sport which I have done.
I know the pain that has to be gone through,
Before you can punch the air and say I've won.

To the velodrome it's pursuit race time.
Three lady cyclists in a line,
Wheel on wheel looking fine.
From the front they look as one,
With just one thought from the gun,
To beat the clock in record time,
When the three of them cross the line.
Feet clamped to pedals whirring round
One slip and all will hit the ground,
On the bend leader swings up high
Then drops down behind, while the others try
To increase their speed and onward fly.
Round on round they speed apace
Against the digital stopwatch race,
Concentration shutting out the pain
Ride for each other, glory to gain,
Swap on swap each other pacing
Lungs on fire hearts are racing
Legs are burning arms are aching
History is in the making,
Six times they ride, six records smashed
Will that ever be surpassed?

It doesn't matter what sport it is.
Whether in hall, on pitch, track, road or water,
These girls give it everything they've got,
Stand to, give no ground or quarter.

So well done girls, you've done us proud,
And we're as chuffed as we can be.
And we'll raise our male chauvinist glasses,
And shout "Well done girls of team G.B."

HEAVENLY WORKINGS OUT

We start off working out down the gym,
So we can look good and chat the girls.
We love it, when feeling full of vim
We're showing off our preacher curls.

We proudly puff out our chest
Pectorals straining beneath our vest.
Our vests we buy one size too small,
To display our pecs and lats to all.

With thighs bulging, filling out our shorts
We train for our particular sports.

Is it worth it, all this pain?
As we lift our weights and sweat and strain,
As we puff and pant with might and main,
What will be the ultimate gain?
What will happen, when we're no longer sporty
And have a tendency to become slightly portly?
Will our gym trips become less and less?
When will be that final bench-press
And our dumbbell squats become a wobbly mess?
Will our hand need to be held on the running machine?
Will we become a stumbling has-been?

No! Not us. We'll go on to the end.
Till the heavenly gym instructor for us doth send.
Then in trackies and trainers we're through them pearly gates.
And we'll get St Peter to help us set up the weights.
Then no more will angels be sat twiddling their thumbs,
We'll have 'em working out, and doing bums and tums.
Then we'll be back where we started with a smile and hello,
Chatting the prettiest angels with the shiniest halo.

LAMENT FOR A MANAGER

At this moment in time there isn't one Scottish manager in the Premiership, since Paul Lambert left Aston Villa. No Fergie, no Moysie, no McLeish, no Macs at all.

I have a theory how this has come about. We have a surfeit of foreign players in the Prem many from African nations. Whilst they have a good grasp of English, they struggle with the Scottish inflections and accent. Thus, the manager's game plan doesn't always come across. Resulting in game losses and sackings.

I'll give you an idea of what I mean. This Prem' side is playing Man. United, and the manager, who is Scottish, comes into the changing room just before the game to give his team a pep talk and game plan.

LAMENT FOR A MANAGER

Och! Right! Noo! Gang ye nae mair to be affrighted,
Just faire we're playing Man. United.
Ye ken the plan right from the git gaw.
Get ye stuck in frae the whistle blaw.

Gang ye doon yon wing wi' yon ballie.
Boot i' across an' nod past yon goalie.
That's all thar's to it, like I tol' ye.
That ye canna ken is braw beyon' me.

Have ya'll ett yer haggis an' yon porridge?
Wi' oot yon gid fud ye'll ne'er manage.
Have ya'll had yer wee dram tae ki' ya gangin',
So doon yon touch line yer'll be wangin'.

I've said ma wee bit naw, it's up tae yae,
Get oot there an' hae a good dae.
I've tol' ye clear ye canna be in the dark.
Gae oot thar an' kick 'em off the park.

The team look at him faces shiny black,
All bemused, alas and alack.
I'm afraid as usual they canna ken.
So, they'll just go out and get beat again.

HELL RIDING
(*Tour de France*)

It's the time of year when I tend to be glued t'th telly.
Not Wimbledon or football,
I'm in France, watching men giving push bikes welly.

My God, them fellers are proper men,
Seeking glory on two wheels.
Zipping along near forty miles per hour
Feeling how freedom feels.
One ninety riders in a bunch
It's called the peloton,
Team on team close together,
Each helping team-mates to get on.

Cruising, thirty miles per hour pace,
Each rider keeping his own space.
Though a vital element of the race
Is jockeying for position and place.

A dog shoots out, a rider tumbles
Creating a nasty mishap.
A dozen bods end up on the floor,
A dozen bikes heap like tangled scrap.
Damaged bikes, unhappy blokes
Feet through wheels, broken spokes
Scrawpy elbows, bleeding knees
Broken bones, blood through Lycra soaks.
Renewing wheels
Mechanic dashes
Support team tending
Gravel rashes
Bandaged gladiators
All limbs smarting
Mechanic holds the bike, ready for restarting.

Lucky ones have already scrambled up,
Quick check of bike and man.
Then ignoring cuts and gashes
Get going, soon as they can.
I'm in the saddle, give us a push
We're going, can't lose one sec,
Wobbling off down the road
Though blood's dripping on the deck.

Doctor's car pulls alongside
Window down, hand holds a plaster,
Rider grabs it, slaps it on
Then belts off pedalling even faster.

One hundred and fifty miles a day,
Through valley, hill and town.
Toiling up zigzag mountain roads
Then o'er th' top to career on down.

Two riders in a breakaway,
Each hoping, to be the one to win the day.

Sitting on the crossbar, crouching low
Lessening the wind resistance.
Zooming down the slopes, sixty miles per hour
Eating up the distance.
Then pedalling like the clappers
Slipstreaming, tucking in behind.
Wheel on wheel, nerves of steel,
To danger they are blind.

Trees flashing past
Blur of green
Hedges, fences
Hardly seen
Concentrate, pedal hard
Accelerate, don't retard
Lean the bike
Round the bend
Straighten up
Now the pedals send
Round and round
Faster still
Gather speed
Down the hill
Now on the flat
Glance to the rear
The peloton is close I fear
Just two bikes in tandem race
Muscles burn, pick up the pace
Lungs a' burstin'
Legs a' pumpin'
Breath a' gaspin'
Heart a' thumpin'
Fifty yards to finish line
Then out the slipstream push
And the race is mine.

DREAMS OF A VILLA FAN
(On the Birth of Prince George)

Our Duchess of C, a babby has had,
A little male bantling for the nation.
I hope he's a Villa fan like his dad,
He may help keep us from relegation.

Though I can't really see him donning the claret and blue,
And waddle out the tunnel, the opposition's mouths gaping.
Though 'spose it's possible he could scrawl one in th' net,
Whilst their defence was bowing and scraping.

So let's get him kitted out in the mini-strip Villa's sent him.
In shorts and shirt of claret and blue.
Though I hope the shorts have got room for a nappy.
We don't want the centre spot covered in poo.

I can just see it there at Wembley,
We've got United in the Charity Shield.
And it's nil-nil at half time,
And we bring Prince Waddler on,
He'd be the tricksyest lad on the field.

With bootees strapped on, he'd bobble the ball along,
And sell their defence dummy after dummy.
Then 'fore we know it, balls in back of th' net,
And he turns, and says, "How's that one mummy?"

So he's got Vidic and Giggsy all banjaxed.
He's done his bit and we're one goal up.
"I'll have to leave you now lads to finish it,
Me mum's callin', with ruskies and milk to sup."

Moyesy shouts, "How did we let that one get by us?"
As he jumps up and down like a loony.
"We should have sent him one of our strips,
Or swapped him for baby Rooney."

You're t' late United, he's a Villa man.
Our team's now got royal blood.
And we can dream of Europe and Champion's League.
By 'eck, wouldn't that be good?

WARS OF THE ROSES (AND STUFF)
1455-1487

Have you ever read about Wars of the Roses
And tried to sort out all the problems it poses?
Why the different factions of Lancaster and York
Were always scrapping, or at least refusing to talk?

And in them days, I'm sure they deliberately played games,
'Cos they had this thing about children's names.
They only knew about two or three,
Like Richard, Edward, John or Henry.

The game was played on purpose, just to confuse
Latter-day scholars, so their brains blew a fuse.
Then history teachers would clock 'em round the ear,
'Cos they couldn't determine or make quite clear
Which Richard, Henry, Edward or John
At what particular time, the throne was sat on.
If William the Conqueror had left us alone,
And not bothered about the English throne.

History then, wouldn't be such a mystery,
And we'd have maintained a continuous dynasty
With lots of good old Saxon names,
Without the "Guess which one I am" games.

We'd have had: Herewards, Edwins, Godwins and Egberts,
Cedrics, Oswins, Swithins and Cuthberts.
We'd have had, Ethalstans and Athalstans, my that could have
been dodgy,
They, along with Osgards and Osgods could confuse the chronology.

But there's loads more of good old Saxon names,
Names for males and names for dames,
Like Offa, Wuffa, Horsa and Hengist.
And names which really the tongue would twist.
You'd think surely there would've been some survivors.
Be good if we had more Lady Godivas!
Ah well, enough of this, I do digress,
Let's get back to the Wars of the Roses mess.

Edward the Third was quite the lad,
Always fighting and scrapping, it made him feel glad.
He did well in France, and bits of it won lots.
Though he too came unstuck when it got to the Scots.
Better leave that particular burden,
Don't want to upset Nicola Sturgeon.

Eddie the Third had twelve kinder, which was nice.
Some of 'em died, and some married once or twice.
His third son had mistresses, that would be John of Gaunt,
Whose progeny and heirs future dynasties would haunt.

One child by his first mistress, seven by his first wife,
Two by his second trouble and strife,
And four by his second mistress Katherine, who became his third wife.
After that he must have been introduced to the knife.
Now, Edward the Third's eldest son was called The Black Prince,

Good warrior and brave, no words did he mince.
Unfortunately The Black Prince dies, his eldest son too,
Leaving the second son Richard, to do what a man has to do.

Eddie Three eventually moves on, and Richard then, at the
tender age of ten,
Becomes Richard the second, they did that back then.
So you can imagine the squabbling behind the scenes,
As the mighty Lords fought, to make sure he ate his greens.

Time goes on and Richard's not a good King.
This is where, John of Gaunt's lot come in for a fling.
John's eldest son Henry deposes Richard, his cousin.
Moves in on the throne, and dusts off its cushion.
Henry now is Henry the Fourth,
Good lad and strong, of Kingship well worth.

Move on twenty years, his son Henry, is now Henry Five.
Hero of Agincourt, and all that jive.
Henry Five's son by his wife Catherine, is in line to be
Henry Vee One.
But later, didn't cut the mustard as number one son.

Though, at nine months old Henry Vee One was crowned King
'Cos Henry Five died unexpectedly of some unknown thing.
Vee One's mum Catherine was French, and not liked over here,
So trouble was brewing, that was clear.

The Lords again, manoeuvred for the regency to control the land,
Fill their own pockets, and make themselves grand.
They side-lined Queen Catherine, 'cos she was French,
Plonked her on the substitutes' bench.

Then, Yorks and Lancs, faces screwed up, teeth gnashing
Faced up to each other, and started bashing,
Denting each other's helmets and giving bloody noses.
This was the start of the Wars of the Roses.

Meanwhile, Henry Vee One, like Hitler's first rockets
Wandered about aimlessly, but with his hands in his pockets,
'Cept when he married some Margaret girl from France,
Had a son, called him Edward, what else? Fat chance.

Now, Rocket Henry Vee One's missus, French Margaret, took her cue
Started shoving her oar in, like they do,
Lined up with the Lancs, thought that would be best.
But the Yorks co-opted Earl Warwick, with a massive war chest.
But Warwick was fickle, would keep changing sides,
Even treated his daughters like bartered brides.
Then at just seventeen Rocket Henry's son dies in battle.
Now we've no heir, so all cages start to rattle.

Quick word about Warwick, he was a sod,
Made alliances to suit himself, thought he was God.
But now it's muck or nettles, all hats in the ring,
'Cos Rocket Henry's away with the fairies, doing his own thing.
The big prize of Kingship is up for grabs.
Everybody smiles at everybody, whilst everybody's back everybody stabs.

At this moment in time Warwick's in with the Yorks.
Pushing forth a claimant called Edward, to be chief exec at the works.
They depose old Rocket Henry, install Ed as Ed number four.
But Warwick's glass is still half empty, and he wants more.
But he overreaches himself, his bus runs out of track,
And at the Battle of Barnet, he gets stabbed in the back.

For a sec' we'll rewind to Henry Five,
Whose young widow French Catherine, drew men like bees round a hive.
She fancied a young fella, Henry Tudor by name,
Who was really able to light her flame.
They had two Tudor sons, Jasper and Edmund, no less.
Half-brothers to Rocket Henry Vee One, so continues the mess.

Rewind again to John of Gaunt,
Whose progeny I told you, the royal line would haunt.
With his mistress and third wife Katherine, they had a son John Beaufort.
A couple of generations down the line, and we have a
Margaret Beaufort at court.
Unknown to her and everyone else at this time,
Her womb will carry the last hope of the Lancaster line.

Rocket Henry Vee One calls his half-brother Edmund Tudor to court,
Makes him Earl Richmond, and guardian of Margaret Beaufort.

Margaret's an orphan, with oodles of dosh and land.
So Edmund sees his chance, and asks for her hand.
He gets her hand and everything else as well,
And it appears to be a love match, far as we can tell.

Margaret Beaufort's thirteen, Edmund Tudor's twenty four.
She gets pregnant, and he dies, where've we heard that one before?
She gets delivered of a son, shall we call him Henry?
'Cos of names to choose from there's not that many.
Now bear in mind this lad can trace his line
Back to Edward the Third, ain't that fine?

Right! Fast forward, the Yorkists have deposed Rocket Henry Vee One,
Who's now old, and a bit battered in his scone.
Anyway, he dies, probably helped on his way,
By Edward of York, who's now Ed the Fourth, hip, hip hooray.

He's married to Elizabeth Woodville, a right comely lass,
Who's not royal blood, but we'll let that one pass,
'Cos they manage twelve children, so it's a fertile line.
And we'll forget about the bloodline over time.
Two of their kinder, were Princes in the Tower, we heard.
And supposedly bumped off, by Ed's brother, Richard the Third.
But we get ahead of ourselves, that didn't come about
'Till after Edward had died, and it became Richard's shout.

The lads in the tower were never found,
So Richard is King, as there's no-one else around.

Meanwhile overseas, growing up, is Henry the Beaufort stroke Tudor lad.
Who thinks what's going on in England is really bad.
He was sent abroad to be kept safe, out of the way,
'Till he could claim his birth right on some future day.
He thinks "Now's my chance to go home, sort this lot out,
Grab that Richard fella, and give him a clout."

So, over he comes and that's what he does,
'Cos other people think the same and jump on his bus.
And on Bosworth Field Richard meets his match,
Is defeated by Henry, on his own patch.
Now Richard's had his day, though he leaves his mark,
But ends up being buried beneath Leicester City car park.

Then to tidy things up and neaten 'em around,
To Edward the Fourth's daughter Liz, Henry gets himself bound.
Now, we've got ourselves a Henry Seven,
Who's married Elizabeth, and is in seventh heaven.
So that's a good thing, both sides united to date,
And them pair can get going, producing Tudor Henry Eight.

RUNNING ON A SHOESTRING

I'm walking along in the sunshine,
My shoelace has come undone.
Next thing I know, its legs in the air,
And I've landed on me bum.
Oh dear I've had an accident,
What on earth shall I do?
I've banged me bum, and I ache all over.
I'll have to find someone to sue.
I'll have a look on th' telly,
Every other advert's one for th' law,
But I'll need a good 'un to make something of this,
I'll need one who is top drawer.

Right Sir, you've had an accident.
That fact we must not hide.
'Cos we can find some poor sod to blame,
And on their back we all can ride.
We're really good at finding fault,
When actually, there's no fault at all.
And we can make some money here
If you will just play ball.
With human rights and health and safety,
Not forgetting P.C. too,
We'll be O.K. for ever and a day
With the lawyers club E.U.

Now, you're extremely lucky
For we employ a good detective.
It won't be difficult for him to prove
Your shoelace was defective.
They must have used the wrong type of thread,
That's the problem you have got.

So no matter how tight you tied your lace,
It ended up a slip knot.

Now in order to help us with your case,
And to prosecute this disaster,
It would be good, if you only could,
End up with your leg in plaster.
Our detective's very good at this,
And we'll supply the crutch.
He'll just hit your ankle with a hammer,
It won't hurt very much.

Oh 'eck, I'm beginning to wish I hadn't bothered with this,
Just scrambled up and dusted meself down.
I can see, it's going to be me,
Who'll end up being shaken down.

Sir, are you clear on this
Before we go through all the stages?
We'll get a few bob for the ankle job,
And some for your lost wages.

What's that you say? How much for you?
Sir, are you trying to be funny?
Your bit is the hurt and pain,
But we get to keep the money.

POOR LAWYERS

We haven't had one for a week or two,
And lawyers will be getting skint.
So we'd better, dream up an excuse for another inquiry,
Then judges, suits and wigs, another mint can print.

Who pays for all these inquiries?
To find out, you don't have too far to go.
Who's got the deepest pocket?
Which can be picked by people in the know.

You're right! It's the taxpayer.
The one, who has no say what his money's spent on.
Who picks the pocket? You're right again.
The suits and wigs of law's higher echelon.

Let's see if we can work out,
Just how the system works.
How we so easily manage to get duped,
By these shiny shoed suited berks.
First of all we pick a scandal.
One that won't drop lawyers or government in a mess.
Say, an unfortunate accident, or a murder,
Shipman, 'phone hacking, or even the good old N.H.S.

Shipman, phone hacking and Stafford Hospital
Are really good ones to pick.
'Cos they're more or less open ended.
Also, on bosses not much mud will stick.

This means the bods at the top,
Will let it run and run.
With no danger of them having to be up front
And face the firing gun.

This is because, staff lower down the line,
Will be the ones to take the flack.
And no-one cares if they carry the can
And get stabbed in the back.
Therefore, the cash cow can be milked on and on,
For ever and a day.
So, raise a cheer for inquiries chaps,
Shout hip, hip, hooray
And give salute to that fine old line,
Let's give it usage one more time
You scratch my back and I'll scratch thine.

When we've picked our inquiry to hide inside,
We must make sure its remit is wide.
The findings then may be inconclusive,
But to our high style of living be conducive.
'Cos it means that then, we can stretch it out for years.
Reducing the thinking taxpayer to tears.

So, wouldn't it be nice? But I wonder if they dare,
To have an inquiry into inquiries, just to show that they care.
And to prove that it's not a complete charade,
(Which I have to say would be really hard),
They could work pro-bono, without a fee.
But that's a step forward I don't think we'll see.

OF TIES AND MEN

What is it with these politicians?
Especially the male variety.
Don't they know that wearing a tie
Bestows a certain sobriety.

Sobriety is what they need; oh aye
To look sincere and erudite to our eye.
But sobriety it must be stressed,
Falls flat, when going about half dressed.
Open necked, without a tie.

Don't they just make you laugh.
They drop the biggest clanger and gaffe
Then think we'll forget and forgive by and by,
No matter how many fingers they've had in the pie.
If they appear now and then, without a tie.

What is it with this non-tie wearing?
When they've washed us, wrung us, hung us out to dry,
Do they think we'll be more forbearing?
Though they've taxed us to the hilt sky high,
If they just go walkabout, without a tie.

And I don't know what their wives are thinking,
Letting 'em loose in a morning with sleep in their eye,
And looking like they've been out all night drinking
As they head off for an interview at Beeb or Sky,
Open necked, without a tie.
Do they think open neck will take the chalk?
As they sashay down the political catwalk.

Each trying to look like an alright guy.
I's 'nuff to make you want to cry,
Looking at 'em half dressed, without a tie.

If they must go about wi' nowt around their neck
Making us embarrassed for 'em, then flippin' eck
For goodness sake, don't wear a whistle and flute
Wear something more appropriate, like a onesie suit.

You don't see the lady M.Ps trying to be something they're not,
Dressing down, looking a clot,
And going about in curlers with headscarves in a knot.
They look good, act the part, and have no need to try,
To look like one of the lads, without a tie.

OF BUSES AND ROUTES VARIOUS

Career politicians are not same as us.
We don't even travel on the same bus.
We definitely didn't start from the same terminus,
'Cos their schools had computers, whilst we had an abacus.
There again, using an abacus or working a slide rule,
Requires intelligence and nous
You're definitely no fool.
A computer makes it all easy seem,
Push the buttons and read the screen.
I think that says a lot for the shower we've got,
Though they can push our buttons, they don't seem to read our screen.

So they can do half the job, but that's as far as they go.
It's not that they're thick or even slow.
They just don't care which way we want our bus to go.

So, let's continue with our little analogy,
Our bus has stopped, so it seems to me.
Theirs has gone on careering along,
Whilst they drink their champers, and sing their songs.
I'm not quite sure what song their singing,
As on their way they're merrily winging.
It's not Rule Britannia, or God Save the Queen,
It could be The Marseillaise, or even Lilli Marlene.

Their eyes are focussed on their ultimate goal.
For which they're prepared to sell our soul,

To buy a ticket to ride for E.U. riches and fame,
But who for that should take the blame?
I'm afraid a lot of it's down to us.
We've let 'em jolly along too long on their E.U. bus.

We should have whipped the wheels off a couple of decades ago,
And made 'em stay at home and run our show.
Then we might have all been on the same bus,
With everyone choosing the route to an agreed terminus.
But now they're on their route with their own timetable,
Our bus seems to have conked, and is back in the stable.
So how to get it going and devise our own bus route?
With our own driver and conductor and bus stops to boot.
That's the difficult bit, to come up with a solution,
To get back on track without resorting to revolution.

MARCH OF THE JACKBOOT

So, they think they've got us, this domineering E.U.
They think to their goose we'll not say, "Boo".
Not so! Not so! The people shout.
Back off! Back off! You assume too much clout.
You interfere too much in private interaction,
And create too much paper in business transaction.
We didn't vote for you to lord it around,
Treading our freedoms into the ground.
To make our every action a dictated motion,
And our every thought a subservient notion.

With diktat in hand, you've stealthily crept,
Turning dreams into nightmares as in innocence we slept.
Making our Parliament a joke, a weak rubber stamp.
As in your shiny jackboots over our courts you tramp.
Democracy's fading, it breathes its last breath,
As the plague from the East creeps on like the Black Death.
"Bring out your dead rights", the cart drivers yell,
Your expired common sense usage and your free speech as well.
Your past ways of working without silly obstruction
All gone away now with E.U. laws introduction.

The "Common Market" idea was not a bad thing,
Just trading as partners, wealth to each to bring.
But like everything good you've taken it too far,
Given yourselves soft jobs and a fancy car.
Bereft of credibility, we're just left to grieve
On your incredible expenses which we can't believe.
But no more will we give into your court's law,
We'll yet snatch our freedom from E.U's. maw.
Our own courts and laws we'll not gainsay,
But of yours, we've had enough, so pack up go away.

GRUMPY OLD ENGLISHMAN

What are they doing to you and me?
What have they done to our poor old country?
That Scottish clown Gordon Mac Brown
Ran the country's finances down.
And Tony Blair, let's be fair
Only had one thought and care.
Self-aggrandizement, and enrichment of his life.
And we had to put up with his grasping wife.
Working the system, working the courts,
Making a packet through E.U.'s human rights racket,
Preferring criminals, foreigners and all undeserving sorts.

Although, when it comes to making a packet working a racket
It's hard for this present lot to be beaten.
And, though their brains were washed down the loos of Eton,
And they can't see past their nose on any topic,
And it appears that they're completely myopic,
When it comes to the rights and preferences of the English man,
They can see well enough to stuff them down the can.

But, they can't see bending over backwards to serve minority factions
Breeds in us mainstream bods bitter reactions.
And looking for someone to stick up for the English race
Drives us into U.K.I.P.'s loving embrace.
And that, if that doesn't work, there's only one solution,
We'll have to have a revolution.

1914 PROLOGUE

Great Britain enters the war 4th of August 1914. Kitchener, (war secretary), calls for volunteers. 350,000 sign up in August. 450,000 in September. Kitchener, foresaw a war of attrition, unlike many others, both British and German, who thought it would be over by Christmas.

These recruits would not enter the war until the battle of Loos in summer 1915. Although I have taken the liberty of placing my two volunteers at the 1st battle of Ypres in November 1914. By then, most of the original British Expeditionary Force, 100,000 men (which was a quarter of the British regular army) was wiped out, being replaced by regular soldiers, colonial troops, and Territorials.

The Maxim design machine gun was employed by the main belligerent countries. The British version named after its manufacturers, Vickers, and the German version named after its place of manufacture, Spandau.

In a cross fire situation each of these killing machines could lay down an effective curtain of fire of about 400 rounds per minute, through which the advancing soldiers were expected to walk. The Maxim was accurate at one and a quarter miles, and effective up to two and a quarter.

The men waiting in the trenches would know all about this, and the British and French tactics of offensive operations made them vulnerable to the exceptional defensive capabilities of this machine gun.

1914 AND ALL THAT
(*August to November*)

'Eh up Jack, are yer comin' wi' me?
I'm joinin' up in the blasted Army.
Off to France for a bit of fun.
It'll beat workin' fer a bit, an' yer'll get to fire a gun.

Nay lad, I dunna fancy much the fightin' bit.
It's not that I'm scared or th' least bit frit,
But I've just got wed and there's a bab on th' way.
Don't think the wife'd like it if I went away.

Aw c'mon Jack, we won't be gone long.
We'll be back be Christmas for a good ole sing song.
'Ave a last fling, afore yer settle down,
An' yer stuck 'ere, floggin' yersen in this bloody factory town.

Aw right then lad, yer've talked me round.
I fancy seein' a bit of foreign ground.
An' th' Missus'll be proud o' me marchin' through th' town,
Wi' me rifle, boots, puttees and khaki brown.
Bloody Hell Jack, it's November already,
An' we're bogged down 'ere at Ypres.
We've seen plenty of foreign ground,
Though it's bin somewhat flung around,
An' now it's lyin' about in great 'eaps.

'eaps made taller by trenches goin' down deep.
An' I can't remember when I last 'ad a decent sleep.
An' me boots are wet an' me socks are soggy.
There's no solid ground, everything's boggy.

Talkin' of bogs, I'll 'ave to go quick.
I've got trench foot, diarrhoea, an' I'm feeling sick.
I 'ope it's still where it was when I went last,
And Jerry's not blown it up with a bloody shell blast.
Trouble with these trenches is, y' need a map
Just t' find a bog, an' 'ave a crap.

Jack, why did I let yer talk me into comin' over 'ere?
It couldn't 'ave been my idea. 'Ad we 'ad t' much beer?
Bloody Hell Jack, this Ypres thing's fair goin' on.
An' the regular British Army, mostly, it's gone.
Blown to Hell in smithereens.
What once was lads, now memories 'as-beens.
Us Kitchener recruits, we're 'olding the line,
But, it's gettin' t' me, an' I'm not feelin' fine.

I'm cold an' I'm wet, an' I'm cheesed off wi' bein' shot at.
An' as fer that sergeant, am I th' on'y one bein' got at?
If 'e prods me again wi' 'is bayonet, t' push me o'er th' top,
I swear I'll 'ave 'im, 'e's one f' th' chop.

Words out Jack, we're o'er th' top at first light.
I don't wanna go Jack, I don't wanna fight.
We won't get a wink o' sleep tonight,
Wi' our guns shellin' 'em, tryin' t' blow 'em t' shite.
An' we know damn well as soon as they stop,
That the Hun wi' the machine gun o'er th' top will up pop.

I don't wanna go Jack, I don't wanna fight.
I don't wanna go o'er th' top at first light.
I'll kill that bloody sergeant if 'e prods me in th' back.
Yer'll,- stick wi' me though?- Won't yer Jack?

I don't wanna go Jack, I don't wanna fight.
I don't wanna go o'er th' top at first light.
It's not bloody fightin' Jack, it's bloody slaughter.
Men doin' to men what they shouldn't oughter.
Once o'er th' top Jack, we won't 'ave much chance.
We'll step an' we'll stumble t' death's final dance.
We'll dance a dance grotesque t' th' Maxim's tune,
Slaves t' chance, an' th' wheel o' fortune.
But, we'll mek' it through? Yer'll watch me back?
Yer'll stick wi' me though? Won't yer Jack?

Our barrage 'as stopped Jack, it won't be long
Afore that blasted whistle blows our swan song.
But we'll be awright Jack? We'll mek it, 'ey?
We'll get through it, t' see another day?

Bloody whistles gone, it's up an' o'er Jack,
Afore that bugger prods me in th' back.
Christ! That Maxim's already started its deathly stutter.
Me stomach's meltin', an' me 'earts aflutter
I'm sloshin' through mud Jack, fallin' in shell 'oles an' stuff.
'Member, when drinkin' at 'ome Jack, we'd joke
We'd be glad when we'd 'ad enough?
Well, I've 'ad enough o' this Jack, I can't stand no more,
I've 'ad enough of bein' plastered wi' others' blood an' gore.

Me 'eads gone Jack, I'm screamin' an' yellin'.
I can see their lines, they'll soon know what I'm sellin'.
I'm gettin' closer, I've one up th' spout Jack.
I can see th' Maxim's flashes from its muzzle black.
I'll 'ave 'im yet Jack, I'll get revenge f' you.
I know it was me talked yer inter this devil's brew.
I'll 'ave 'im yet Jack, don't you fret.
I've just got t' get a bit closer yet.

Oh! Bloody Hell tha'r'urts, an' I'm grovellin' in th' mud.
Me guts is showin' Jack, an' I'm pourin' blood.
The bastard's got me, cut me near in two.
It'll not be long Jack, afore I'll be wi' you.

NOT SO FUNNY EXCURSION
(Prologue)

All great works of art, in whatever field, promote inspiration in others; to emulate it, or use it as a springboard for their own efforts, whether the endeavour in question is on canvas, stage, written or sculpted.

Dante's Divine Comedy is one such work. It has inspired much, especially in the world of canvas, and sculpture.

Very briefly, the poem tells the story of Dante, whom, we are led to believe, has fallen off the Right Path a little, and is now in a dark place. The lovely Beatrice, whom Dante has worshipped from afar is sent to ask Virgil, the long dead Roman poet, to show him the Path back to virtue, God and Heavenly aspirations.

It was written between 1308 and 1320, it took him twelve years. He died one year after its completion, fifty six years old.

The poem comprised 14,233 lines. I haven't read it all, and I think I'd have difficulty appreciating it if I tried, more, through my ignorance, than any lack of merit on Dante's part. It was the first literary work at that time in Italy, to be written in the vernacular of the day, rather than classic Latin. An innovation of its time.

I have respectfully taken synopses I have read, and relevant verses of the poem another step in that direction, and trust the great man will not be too upset with my humble efforts.

The original story is allegorical in so much that it parallels a Christian's journey towards God, as seen by the medieval world.

NOT SO FUNNY EXCURSION

How on earth did I get in this Dark Wood?
P'raps 'cos I'm not treading the Right Path, the Path that's Good.
I'm thirty five, it feels like I'm alive,
And I'm only half way through my span of years,
Why am I now, having to plough, my path through this dark valley of tears.

But hold! Yonder hill top, it catches the sun.
I must climb towards its heavenly light.
And now my journey I've begun,
I hope the way I'm heading is right.
Suddenly, my way is barred by a snarling leopard,
And I must turn aside.
Only to encounter a lion twice as big,
My God I could have died.

I turn again on another route, to gain my desired objective,
My way is blocked once more, therefore I am sure
This computer game must be defective.

For I am forced back by a she-wolf,
Back into this dark wooded vale.
I'm on a loser, you can bet on it.
For there's no way past a stroppy female.

Head in hands, I despair, all is care and woes.
But, then I pull myself together,
And on a tissue blow my nose.

I see a figure walking towards me,
Across this darkened glade.
I know that face, I've seen the death mask,
It is the poet Virgil's shade.

"Hail fellow, well met", I call, "I'm afraid I'm in a bit of a lurch,
For a way out of this God forsaken hole, I am trying to search."
"Best find another way, Dante old mate,
That she-wolf will have you and me as well.
But, being as you're here, come along with me,
And I'll show you around Heaven, Purgatory, and Hell."

It's Good Friday evening and the two of us
Are approaching Hell's entrance gate.
I say, "Hey hold up! Hang on a mo', just wait.
Am I worthy of this guided tour,
Virgil, my old mate?"

"'Course you are, of that I'm sure,
Think not you are of stature poor,
That you're not equal to Aeneas or St Paul,
And not comparable to them at all.
Don't worry Dante, down there you'll be a hit.
And you remember the lovely Beatrice, who was your fancy bit?
Well! The one you courtly loved from afar,
And to whom you hitched your worshipping star.
St Lucia sent her to me, your sorry plight to ease,
She said, "Virge, will you do it for me please?
Show him the Right Path, from the Dark Woods,
'Cos he's not a bad lad really, in fact, I think he's the goods.
So, just think Dante, with a bit more bottle,
You could have made her your study,
Instead of Aristotle.
Therefore, have courage Dante.
For there's three heavenly women playing on your side.
And with me as guide, what can go wrong?
Come on along, enjoy the ride."

It won't take much, good listener, of your imagination,
To appreciate my overwhelming fear,
Coupled with feelings of trepidation.

So as we approach the entrance and Hell's unholy portal,
My anxiety is running riot, 'cos as yet I am still mortal.

We're through the gate,
And you'll be pleased to note,
That I haven't yet
Learned this tale by rote.
And I'll have to gloss over the gratuitous violence,
Or I'll put at risk my poetic licence.
Though restrictions on time, quills and paper exist,
I think, of the elements you'll get the gist.

Down here there's no blanket punishment for our misdeeds,
The penance reflects Satan's sadistic needs.
Each sin is mirrored in the Seven Deadly's retribution scenes.
So maximum vindictiveness from it he gleans.

I think somewhere down here; they're able to get Film4 on telly,
And Satan's been viewing, whilst chewing, on mortal tasties from his deli.
And he's seen Brad Pitt, and Morgan Freeman, in the film titled "Seven".
Which is about the furthest you can get, from anywhere like Heaven.
So, he's modelled his punishment block on that movie.
I bet he's really chuffed with himself, thinks it's fine and groovie.

There's Pride, Greed, Anger, Gluttony, Envy, Sloth, and Lust.
Play any of those cards from your hand, and your flush'll be bust.
And any of them, your chances of Heaven will ruin,
Which just about kicks into touch, anything on Earth worth doin'.

Anyway, me and Virge we've seen the lot.
We've seen poor souls wallowing
In all sorts of rubbish and snot.
We've ridden on centaurs' backs,
Over sinners drowning in boiling blood,
We've been carried about by monsters,
That bit was good.
We've seen poor souls being cooked in boiling pitch.

And souls with heads back to front,
Not knowing any way from which.
Priests upside down in holes,
In a situation dire,
But making smashin' Roman candles,
'Cos their feet were on fire.

We've seen souls turned into trees,
With boughs that snap and bleed.
And harpies, which on anything will feed.

We chatted with lost souls,
One or two of 'em me muckers.
And some of 'em popes, priests, kings or vicars.
Makes you wonder what on earth's going on up there?
Does anyone make it to the Penthouse, God's glory to share?
Or, are they all down here suffering something awful,
For going against holy commands, and doing stuff unlawful?

On the last level, bods are encased in ice,
Just their heads are showing.
And keeping stuff frozen
Is a sub-zero wind,
Which is from somewhere blowing.

To cap it all, we've just seen Satan an' all,
And he too is bound round his waist in ice.
An' it's him flapping his wings,
Great leathery things,
That's keeping everything cold, and not nice.

I tuck up close behind Virge, so as to hide and keep warm.
As carefully on tip-toe we sneak past Satan's terrible form.
Satan has three faces, and each mouth chews on a sinner.
Today, he's having Judas Iscariot, Brutus and Cassius for dinner.

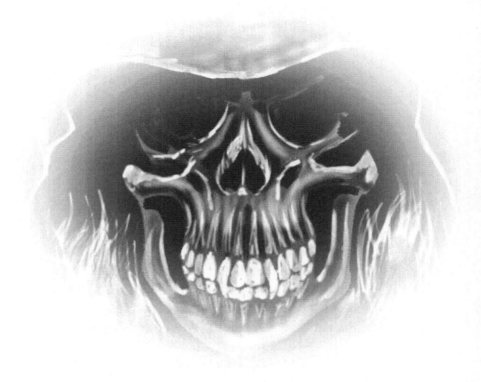

Now at last, we're safely past,
And can continue with our story.
The next stop on our itinerary,
Is a resort called Purgatory.

In keeping with human nature,
We find Purgatory not so interesting.
'Cos most souls there have bottled out,
And confessed their sins when things got testing.

So instead of being permanently in Hell burning,
This lot, how to be teacher's pets are learning.
And each soul, once again a Sunday school student.
Which, when considering the alternative,
Would be sensibly prudent.
So, they work their way through Purgatory, suitably penitent,

Hoping the headmaster will spot their devotions,
And towards them relent.
Then they eventually will attain cap and gown,
And sing praises forever, and not be sent back down
To that place below, of which we spoke,
Which let's face it, is no joke.

Now Dante is progressing nicely through Purgatory,
And we're coming to the end of our story.
The next step is Heaven, where Virgil can't go.
This is where; dare I say it; sex begins to show.
For the lovely Beatrice becomes Dante's guide.
But have no fear, their love is pure and they've nowt to hide.
And it's only cynical sods like me at all,
Who think, "Hey up! Are they about to fall?"
But no! Dante's sins are purged, the banners unfurled.
God's in his Heaven, all's right with the world.

WHITECHAPEL PROLOGUE

Whitechapel, an area of East London and a boil on the backside of the city. An area of mixed class with middle classes living cheek by jowl with poverty struck poor.

In the middle to late eighteen hundreds the main roads were not particularly squalid. The greatest suffering, filth, abject poverty, prostitution and crime, were reserved for the warrens of narrow dark streets, with their dilapidated housing, which branched off these more affluent thoroughfares.

At this time, the population of these warrens was swollen to bursting by immigration from Ireland, and Jewish immigrants from Europe and Russia fleeing persecution. (What's changed?) Sometimes they would be living nine or more to a room.

It's easy to imagine in these areas, ignored by the rich West End, that an atmosphere of self-regulation prevailed. Maybe, even local justice.

It is with this in mind, that I submit the following theory on the Jack the Ripper mystery.

WHITECHAPEL

It is full night, and the wraithly mist from London's rivers shows to
the moon its wispy strands.
The moon a disc, dimly seen, smudged with gas light's echo thrown
back from chimney'd smoke and foggy bands.
The fetid river mist, miasma'd more by broken drains unrepaired by
navvies shovel
Swirls around the gas lamp bracketed on the alley's corner hovel.
Its uncertain light falls upon the drunks pitched from the bawdy
ale house, who now in the gutters grovel.

It's Whitechapel, in the year eighteen eighty eight.
The spectre of the Ripper affrights the women working their nightly
trade out late.
But work they must, to win the tabled bread for kin,
And buy the gin, that lifts them from their hungered gloom,
And pays the rent on a damp and ratty room.

I am now the eldest daughter, since my sister was beguiled
By one she thought might be a friend,
But misled her to a tragic end.
My father, from foul disease which almost left him dead
Can no longer work to earn the family bread.
My mother, a seamstress can no more ply her trade,
Her tuberculous lungs hacking her into a nebulous shade.

I must go out this night, and stand beneath the alley corner light.
My father spoke me stern, and made me whore-ish gestures learn.
My mother, in between hawking bloody phlegm, would sew my
dress with stitch and hem.

I have been rehearsed, I am well versed in what I am to do.
I'll wrest that gentried sovereign father from gentried purse for you.

I am in place beneath the corner light, standing in coquettish pose,
but, afeared of what I may be later doin'.
Nearby the jangly ale house piano accompanies raucous songs and
doses of mother's ruin.

I shiver in the night's clammy misty air, my thoughts a jumble
As through the fog I strive to see with piercing stare.

Now, muffled, coming through the self-same fog,
I catch the sound of jingly harness and the clop of horses jog.
All mingled with the clatter of an approaching Hansom's wheels.
I wonder if this is how a soldier feels?
Before the charge, before the fight, will I be alright?
Or is this my life on Earth's last night?

Out of the fog the Hansom cab appears.
Muffled up cabbie, hand on whip,
Cab swaying like some land borne ship.
Horse sweeps past, eyes glaring, snorting, nostrils flaring as on the
bit it champs,
Then the driver in a blur, then the lighted trap lamps.

The way is narrow, I lurch for safety back flat against the wall,
I have no wish to 'neath the horse nor carriage fall.
Then through the fog bloomed window of the cab door I see,
A top-hatted toff who stares at me.
A cane raps hard upon the carriage roof,
The cabbie slows then stops, now no sound of wheel no sound of hoof.

Cab sways as the toff alights. Horse snorts and stamps a foot.
Top hat, silk scarf, and opera cloak generate a turgid feeling in my gut.

He carries a gold topped cane and leather bag, the cab moves off and
morphs into the mist.
I must play the part for which I'm coached, too late now to run or to resist.
Pert pose presented, I recite my line with complimentary provocative mime.
"Evenin' dearie. Lookin' fer a good time?"
He faces up to me, bag and cane upon the ground, now having both
hands free.
He o'er me looms, I look up at him, his features pale in lighting dim.
Eyes black as coal, thin lips, long nose,
Top hat me full o'ershadows.
He reaches out, my heart goes cold
He presses on me one sovereign gold.

A sovereign gold from loaded purse,
I must remember now in what I'm versed.
He must sense my fear and feel my trembling,
Though I trust, no hint of my dissembling.
No word between us, his hand on my shoulder,
My God, that I was feeling bolder.
Fingers dig into my flesh, no chance to run.

Is now the final act begun?
I am guided down the alleyway.
A gully dark, even in the day.
Against a slimy wall I'm roughly thrust,
Two hands reach out towards my bust,
His fingers fumble at my buttons, sweat glistens on his brow.
I must react, I am undone, if I don't do it now.
Reaching behind my dress, to Mother's secret seams, I feel,
And grasp the hilt of my stiletto steel.
Now the action much rehearsed,
In which my Father had me right versed.
An upward thrust with all my strength,
The blade's pushed up and under ribs full length.
His head snaps back with a start,
My steel has pierced his evil heart.
His mouth drops open, his eyes roll up, then with not a sound
He crumples up upon the ground.

From out the mist menfolk gather, feeling bolder,
The corpse dragged up and heaved on many a manly shoulder.
This night the Thames' fast tidal race it will receive.
No grave for him, no mourners, none for him to grieve.
Wrapped up in canvas, with bag and cane,
Well weighted down, ne'er to be seen again.
The purse of sovereigns shared out around,
This day, bread on tables will be found.
No more victims, no more cadavers
O'er which the sweating beast ere slavers.
My sister now avenged will be,
Her spirit soaring, flying free,
Retribution claimed, justice done,
And London's greatest mystery just begun.

ALL HALLOWS' EVENING
October 1958

I am holidaying alone,
I need to be on my own.
A refugee from an acrimonious divorce.
Unfit to give recourse to genuine remorse
When, Anne, my wife, did die of a broken heart,
As I was to blame in no small part.

My current love thought it best,
From each other to have a little break,
A short rest apart, some time to take,
To ascertain the feelings of our heart.

So, out in the sticks I rented this cottage small,
One up, one down, and hardly any amenities at all.
What did exist, were in a lean-to out-house.
Hardly enough room in all to house a mouse.
Two miles away, the nearest habitation,
A village where, a public house the only recreation.
But it suited in my situation.
Time for reflection and a little meditation.

For long days, I'd find myself local footpaths treading.
Seeking a tranquil mind and peaceful situation.
Then at eventide from my cottage to the village heading,
Towards my nightly repast, and recreation.

Sometimes nipping through a field gate I'd take a shortcut where,
I'd pass the farmer's guardian, a scarecrow,
A solitary sentry rooted there, surveying ground now cold and bare.
Straw bonnet on straw hair,
Hollowed out turnip head, eyes, nose, mouth, formed with care.

This one a female crop protector, long sleeved blouse and stripy skirt.
Just planted there, guarding two acres of now empty dirt.
Glancing at her as I make my way towards the hedgerow stile,
I could not but notice her strangely sardonic smile.

Now, onward over fields all stubble ploughed.
I'd then clamber gates, and vault the churchyard wall with ivy
well-endowed,
Thread my way past lopsided tomb stones planted in the grass,
Through the lychgate, across the road, and through the pub's door pass.

A pint of the landlord's best in my hand,
My back to the fire now I stand,
Perusing the house bill of fare,
I dine well, then an evening with the locals share.
Cards, darts, bar-skittles, verbal banter as well,
But all too soon rings the last orders bell.

Sup up, coat on, reluctantly farewells spoken,
I'm through the door, the pleasant evenings spell now broken.
Ye gods, it's blasted cold out here.
The night is full mooned, frosty, starry clear.

I see my breath in wisps before me in the wintry air.
I'll take the short cut if I dare.

'Course I dare, the moonlight's bright as day,
No chance that I will lose my way.

I re-cross the road, and through the lychgate pass,
Thread through the graveyard guardians planted in the grass.
I now recall it's Halloween.
I glance nervously about, though there's not one gaping tomb to be seen.
No rotting corpse from interment climbing,
Moaning, groaning, mouth open gaping miming.
I give a laugh, but quicken my pace away from all,
And then gladly vault the churchyard wall.

Onward again over fields ploughed stubble,
My breath billowing in front like a cartoonist's bubble.
I know the next bit's easier, as over the stile I go,
And start to cross the home of the rooted scarecrow.

My attention is grabbed as I see, a yellow glow in front of me.
I stop that abruptly I almost slip.
The glow is from the scarecrow's turnip.
Of course, because it's Halloween,
Some soul cakers to light a candle have been.
I draw level, and look close into those turnip eyes.
But then conclude with some surprise,
I can't see a candle, I must confess,
I suppose it to be well hidden by her dress.

It's cold, I must press on home to light a fire.
And a couple of whiskies with hot water ere I retire.

In the cottage by a blazing fire, comfy in my armchair,
A glass of whisky at my side, I feel relaxed, no care.
I lean back sleepy, the fire dies, an owl its nightly haunting flies,
But I sleep on, my book unread falls from knee to floor.
Then, I am snatched awake by a noise outside the out-house door.

I lurch up from my chair,
Open the living room door, and look into the out-house, where,
Outside I see a face, a face quite clear,
A turnip face with glowing eyes, triangular nose, and mouth fixed
in sardonic sneer,
A straw bonnet, set upon straw hair, a long sleeved blouse and stripy skirt.
I try not to believe what I see, but I know this thing wants to do me hurt.

A gloved hand filled with straw,
Hammers against, and breaks the glass set in the door.
The turnip head, candle like light shining from within,
Which lights the eyes, and makes grotesque the mocking malevolent grin
Nods to me, I slam the door and flee

Across the room, out the front and down the garden path.
My God! This is impossible, whoever heard of a scarecrow psychopath.

I bolt down the road towards the village.
What's chasing me I daren't envisage,
But chasing me it surely is, and terror my sanity is unseating.
As behind me, gaining, I hear clumpy straw filled shoes upon the
roadway beating.
The gateway comes up on my left, I'm through it,
In the field I'll surely have more chance,
To out-manoeuvre in this nightmare dance.
Terror makes me glance around,
To find she is gaining ground.
With arms out wide, straight legged she strides in alternate obscene jerks
I am terrified and horror struck, about to go berserk.
Oh! Things are changing, I am stiffening, slowing, seizing.
Fingers stick out straight, arms forced out wide, knee joints locking, freezing.
I am static, locked solid, the only thing to move, my eyes.
And when two straw filled arms wrap around me, I am petrified but
not surprised.
My captor carries me with ease across the ground,
And plants me on that self-same spot, to which she once was bound.
I cannot move, I can only think and see.
My thoughts and sight the only senses left to me.

My persecutor moves around into my field of vision
And stands there arrogant, upon the completion of her mission.
A mission though, not yet quite complete,
She is not yet with vengeance filled, replete.
As I watch, her visage changes, her limbs and features soften.
Gone is the turnip and straw hair, I now look upon a face seen often.
Anne! My erstwhile wife, whom I by mental cruelty slayed.
Has returned to steal my life, whilst I the price for treachery have paid.

As I look at her transformed, I see her as she was when first we met.
I am o'ercome too late, with sad remorse and delayed regret.

She mocks me now, and with arms outstretched, completes a graceful
pirouette.
And the woman who was once my wife
Walks away to the cottage, and takes with her my life.

Meanwhile. What of me? What is my fate? Now here I stand
With straw filled body legs and hands.
With turnip head and hair of straw.
What am I here now for?

Unlike my wife,
Who innocent was able to reclaim her life,
I am left to hunger after mine in this raggy state.
Until, I, like her encounter someone warped by hate.
And only then perhaps, escape this catatonic state.

But I am here until at least next year,
And 'til some wayfarer comes by, who has been it's clear
To his or her spouse unfaithful, and has used them ill and mean
Then, I uprooted will be, and will walk again on Halloween.

MOLAR MINDING

My dental check-up was due last week.
Whilst waiting, took a book to read,
To shut my mind, and distract my attention
From the sound of a drill going at speed.

I seemed to be waiting, sat there ages,
Though I hadn't read many pages,
When my name was called by the nurse.
Up I stood, lips tightly pursed.
Full of trepidation
Anticipating the worst.

Out came the bloke before me,
Like a shot from a gun,
Looks like what went on in there
Wasn't that much fun.

Mouthing thankyous - goodbyes mumbled.
Took one look at his face,
Thought - should I about turn and exit the place?
No sooner thought, the idea rejected,
I was only there to have teeth inspected.

Smiley dentist - "You O.K. today?"
Me wishing I was miles away.
Brave face on, stride towards the chair.
Bum barely on the seat, legs flicked in the air,

Eyes dazzled by shining light,
Me trying not to show my fright.
Then it's, - toothpick in, open wide,
Tapping teeth around inside.

One two, three four five, - hope to get out of here alive.
One missing there, six seven eight,
Up to now, we're doing great.

Oh! A little filling there could do with renewing,
O hell! I can feel anxiety brewing.
I know the next thing that he'll say,
"If you don't have a jab, - I'll do it right away"

Conflicting thoughts through my brain,
Shall I go on? And not have to come back again.
Can I stand a bit of pain?

Sweetly smiling dental nurse, - looks me in the eye,
Daring me to go crumply faced, - or to cry.

I acquiesce with sheepish grin,
Oh my God. I've really dropped myself in.
Then he, - with his finest ghoulish expression
Jams safety glasses on me like he's on a mission.

Bib strapped on round my neck.
Drill starts up, - oh flippin' 'eck,
Fingers interlocked beneath the sheet
Muscles tensed, - ready to meet
The expected rush of sound and vibration
The stab of pain through the drill's rotation.
Open wide. Oh dearie me
Drill is screaming like a banshee.

There's sucker, - fingers, - drill and mirror inside
(Can't be no room for owt-else besides.)
Bits of everything flying free
Bits of filling bits of me

Bits I hope don't really matter
Bits that on my glasses spatter.

All at once I've an empty gob
Right! That's that part of the job.

Open wide again, nurse starts mixing
Inside me metal stuff he's fixing,
Clamps and screws and dental parts.
This, - is, - then, - when he starts.

"Where are you going for your holidays?"
"YAH-YAH-YAH-YAH-YAH" I says.
He says, - "That's good I've been there,
On the beaches girls go topless bare."

"YAH-YAH-YAH-YAH-YAH-YAH-YAH"
"Yeah that's right, we hired a car."

It's obvious to me, - when exams they pass,
Dentists then go on to special language class.

Then after thrutching and pushing with fingers strong,
(Doesn't seem to have been very long),

After tightening clamps and packing and pushing,
We wait while stuff hardens, - no point in rushing.
Then it's slacken off screws and remove the hardware,
Tidy up rough bits with some care.
Then it's, - "Right, wash out that's you done,
Wasn't that a lot of fun?"
May be fun for him, but I didn't think it funny
'Specially as it cost me money.

"Oh! And there's another one there could do with a tweak.
So make an appointment at reception for next week."

REVENGE

A story of love, greed, murder, regret, and revenge. Set in the 1880s, Victorian times, in the family seat of a large estate.

I wake up with a start, wet through with sweat, racing heart.
I lie abed, o'ercome with dread.
The room's ice cold. Oh, not another night
Lying here consumed by fright.

Lying in this very room, where consummated love didst bloom.
My thoughts return to that night
When, o'ercome by rapacious greed love took flight.
Why did I take your life oh loving wife?
Hands about your throat oh dearest heart
Your hazel eyes from their sockets did start,
And question me. Why oh why
Does love's look from your visage fly?
What have I done that you would treat me so?
You, with whom life's tapestry I sought to sew.
How have I sinned? That you dear heart,
Life's loving seams must rip apart.

But I'm committed now.
As from angst ridden furrowed brow
Beads of sweat start down my face.
My teeth clench fast, my heartbeats race.
In my misted greed, your once lovely looks recede
In red veined eyes, you, horror struck, unanswered questions plead.

Your gaping mouth no life giving air can gain.
My thumbs press hard, soon you'll feel no pain.
Screaming silent screams,
You live in fact, a nightmare's dreams.

Now 'tis done, life's flickering candle outed.
But ere the glim is finished
Your now unlovely face accuses me,
Its beauty ravaged now diminished.

In blankets wrapped, I gently laid your body down.
Leaving you to rot beneath unhallowed ground.

Though since my torturous deed, in greed well steeped,
I can no longer sleep, remorse runs deep.
Remorse, which drags my sanity around inside my head,
Crushes it against my skull, numbing all but the pain that you are dead.

I no longer feel the blessing of slumber's soothing kiss.
Flinging back the sheets I stumble from this canopied couch of marital bliss
And thrash wide the drapes excluding the moonlit scene below,
I scan the lawns awash with heavens harsh yet subtle glow.

Lawns beneath which, now you lie abed.
Oh how I wish that you were not yet dead.
That I had not buried you at dead of night beneath that innocent green.
No moon shone on that darkly night, concealing full the shameful scene.

I told your friends that you abroad had gone,
And I was to sell up all, and directly follow on.
Sell this massive landed stately pile,
Then, join you in sunnier climes the while.
I cannot sell, I have not sold.
My hands do not yet grasp stolen gold.

Your spirit holds me to this stately mausoleum.
This vast statued, portraited, galleried family museum.
This place you loved, that I would gain by foul and accurs-ed deed.
The guilt of which, I now, would well be freed.

Though your body rots beneath the lawn-ed soil,
I would hold you close e'en now, if death's clutches we could foil.

Unfast the window, out the bedroom's lofty balcony make a tread.
Glancing down at your clandestine moonlit grave, wishing again that
you were yet undead.
A cloud fronts the moon, for a moment shadowing the luna lit mat of grass.
I glance again, a hand o'er my eyes I pass.

In the distance, two yellow pinpricks dance in tandem.
Thoughts flit through my head, thoughts quite random.
I stare at them, fully fixated, mesmerised, fascinated.
No doubt about it, they're getting nearer,
Encompassed by a wraithlike shape becoming clearer.

Closer still the apparition gets.
Wrapped in a cloak, or, is it blankets.
Seemingly floating in mid-air
All I can do is stand and stare.
Mesmerised by yellow eyes, dancing across the lawn.
My thoughts coalesce, it begins to dawn.
She's coming for me, she loves me still.
I am forgiven for treating her ill.

She rises now, level with the balcony,
Way above the ground, suspended, floating free.

I perceive the grave stink, death's odious smell,
Which strangely attracts, rather than repel.
From wormy aspect, yellow eyes bore into mine.
She whispers, "Come to me one more time."

She floats there, just beyond the balcony rail,
"Come to me my love, do not fail."
I stand upon the rail, no fear have I, for she's my love.
Though from the ground we're way above.

She holds out her arms and smiles from her rotting face,
Eager for me, calling me to her embrace.
I step forward into her open arms, .

Then of a sudden all is alarm.
I'm falling down to the ground, falling but twisting around.
I see a spectral head thrown back before I hit the path,
And the last thing I hear is a mocking spectral laugh.

SPIDER

I'm sent off to bed, I've got a cold, the family's off to the pictures.
But because I'm ill, and not very well, they've placed on me some strictures.
"Get a hot drink, and take that Lemsip, and get yourself off to bed.
And do as you're told, no mooching down here, and watching telly instead."

Would I do that? After what you've said, and well laid down the law.
Now you've gone. Yes I would, I'll please myself, I'm not your cat's paw.

Telly on, snuggle down, in my armchair, wrapped in dressing gown.
Lemsip in hand, whisky chaser to follow,
And maybe another one, just to test my swallow.

Better not have a light on, in case they come back unexpected.
Then I can sneak off to bed quickly, undetected.
'Cos, I'll not hear the last of it for days,
If I don't do exactly as she says.

Now, sitting here in the living room, telly on, flickering in the gloom.
A couple of whiskies, nice and cosy, tucked up warm, feeling dozy.

All at once my attention's caught by,
A movement, in the corner of my eye.
I turn my head towards the door,
To see a big long legg-ed spider on the floor.

My God! He's a size, didn't think they got that big.
He's got more hair on his body than some blokes have on a wig.

I didn't think we had tarantulas over here.
All at once I feel a bit queer.

As I watch transfixed, he does a quick scuttley dash.
God he's quick, quick as a flash.
And his stops are as quick as his starts.
I don't know which affect me most, his instant freezes or sudden darts.
He's that fast when he moves, he disappears from sight,
Then stops, and is visible again, illumined by the telly's light.

Now, he's stationary in the middle of the floor,
Am I imagining it, or has he grown some more?
He certainly looks bigger than before,
When I first saw him by the door.

One that size you couldn't miss around the house,
His body must be as big as a mouse.
I'm feeling now just a little bit wary,
In fact it's getting more than a little bit scary.

Six feet apart we each eyeball, doing the biz.
Two of mine, and six of his.
How is it he's now big enough for me to see his eyes.
God, if he was in a spider show he'd sure win first prize.

Whoops! He's off! Oh heck!
Grab the whisky bottle by the neck.
Sit back in my chair and pull my feet up.
But not before a quick gulp I sup.

Don't panic, he's only a spider and I'm a man.
But this bottles no good, I need a frying pan.
Where's he gone now? There's only one place he can be.
Behind the entertainment unit across from me,
Behind the music centre and the telly.
If I had that pan I could give him a welly.

But from the corner of the room I daren't shift my stare.
Let alone sprint for the door, after getting up from my chair.
I'm feeling edgy, sweating, anxious getting.
I firmly grip the bottle by the neck,
If he appears, I'll hammer him into the deck.

I have to revise that thought, as from above the television set,
A many articulated leg appears, all furry and thicker yet.
Something, somewhere I must have missed.
That leg now is as thick as my wrist,
And of a sudden, another comes into sight.
Which if it was possible doubles my fright.

Both flicker airily, sensing the atmosphere, feeling for me, aware of my fear.
Like a boxer sparring they seek direction,
A prelude to my detection.
In my turmoiled mind I cannot dwell on the hell about to descend on me.
I ineffectually smother my imagination running free, and fail to blot
out the terror about to be,
Blot out the abomination I'm bound to see, that will bring about my
end most hideously.

For that's the ultimate end, my demise.
That conclusion comes as no surprise.
P'raps part devoured now, then what's left dragged away to be entombed
In some secret webby catacomb.

Overhead, leggy shadows flutter across the ceiling.
Terror grips my heart, my head tries disbelieving.

Now, a multi-eyed hideous head appears, with grasping mandibles
Down which saliva dribbles,
Each, either side of a snapping jaw.
I imagine bits of me disappearing in that maw,
Fingers hands toes and feet,
Bits of me, but to him just bits of meat.

I squeeze right up tight in my chair, can't get no further back.
Eyes start wide from my head, jaw drops open, slack,

Hair stands on end, sweat runs down my face,
My pulse beats fast, heart starts to race.

The damn thing's grown massive, fills the corner of the room,
I'm in the shadow of its belly as o'er me it looms.
A belly pulsing, heaving, hairy round and fat,
About to drop on me, and squash me flat.

The stench of hell assaults my senses,
Every muscle in my body tenses.
On six legs it stands, high above my chair.
Its hairy body seems to hover there.
Two legs freely claw at me, one scratchy foot drags through my hair.
I curl up in my chair, striving to escape the tangle
Of legs and mandibles attempting to mangle
Me into the jaws, all gaping, gnashing,
From which onto me stinking saliva is splashing,
I try to scream, but I'm all aquake.
Then the front door bangs and I'm awake.

"I knew you'd be down here, look at the state you're in,
Sweating, shaking, and you can wipe that silly rictus grin,
Looking like some stupid clown,
And, what's that smelly mess splashed down your dressing gown?"

SWIMMING TIME

My joints just like the rest of me, are feeling the stress and strains
Of a working life on the go, and quite a few sporting aches and pains.
To loosen up and get exercise, by going for a swim,
I thought to go to Moss Farm baths, as an extra to Dave's Gym.

For my trunks I searched half an hour or more
In draws and boxes and bags.
But it's so long since I'd seen 'em,
I could have used 'em up for rags.

Oh, I remember now, it's coming back,
Last time I had 'em on,
When I dived in, they came straight off,
'Cos the 'lastic it had gone.

Very embarrassing it was,
Don't laugh, I nearly drowned
Trying to find 'em in the deep end,
On the bottom scrabbling round.

Feeling that this was not for me,
That's the last time I had a swim.
And when I finally got home,
I chucked my bathers in the bin.

It's ages since I swam in Northwich, and my manly phis-que showed.
It was so far back, I shudder to think, it was at Vicky Road.

I wonder what the bath's like now?
But best don't think at all,
Or my resolve will disappear
All melty, like a snowball.

Here we are, we're at it now,
This is the session called liquid lunch.
From twelve till half one, the given slot,
At Moss Farm, here comes the crunch.

A nice lady takes my money,
It costs me three and a half quid.
My God, I don't want to buy the place,
That was not a property bid.

Oh dear, a frosty stare I get.
I hope it's warmer inside.
As I push through the swinging doors
Acting all nonchalant besides.

A blast of hot air hits me now,
My goodness, what a greeting.
I could come down here regular like,
And save a bomb on central heating.

All changed now, gear stowed away,
Feeling snazzy in a cossi that fits.
I patter off towards the deep end.
Trying to look a bit like Mark Spitz.

Stand at the deep end, surveying all,
Folk bobbing up and down, the water churning.
I'm trying to look all professional like,
Not someone who's just relearning.

Some, like torpedoes, semi submerged
Plough up and down the lane.
Should they meet head on, there'll be an explosion,
Each the other trying to blame.

Two lady porpoise, gracefully in tandem
Gossip up and down the bath.
Don't know how they find time to breathe,
They really are a laugh.

Older walruses, who you can tell
Have done a bit an' all,
Sharp angled elbow on the retrieval stroke,
As they demonstrate their crawl.

Come on, get going, I tell myself.
Don't stand there like a dope.
Look like you know what you're doing,
Me, know what I'm doing? Some hope.

Bending down I scoop water up, splashing it over my skin.
Boy, I'm really looking the part, as I prepare to swallow dive in.

Toes grip the edge, adopting a semi crouch,
I'm poised, with arms swept back.
Oops, I overbalance, and belly-flop in.
Hit the water with a smack.

Better stay submerged for a while.
Allow the ignominy to dissipate,
Before I float up towards the surface,
And try to resume a dignified state.

Just then I'm grabbed, there's arms around me.
I feel I'm in a truss.
Something's got me, what's going on?
Can't be a squid or octopus.

The blasted lifeguard's got me now,
He's being overzealous
It must have been my stylish dive,
Hurt his pride, and made him jealous.

He drags me over to the side,
And pitches me on the tiles.
Next thing he's pummelling me on the back.
Whilst all around are wreathed in smiles.

I'm sure he's jumping on me,
As I lie in recovery pose.
My head keeps banging on the floor,
And water is flooding down my nose.

"Are you alright?" He asks solicitously.
"Course I am", as I turn towards him frowning.
"I'm glad about that," he smilingly says.
"'Cos you sure looked like you were drowning."

I'm standing there all sheepish like,
Dripping in a puddle.
Seeing all the women round about,
Giggling in a huddle.

Feeling a proper ninny,
Off to cubicle changing I creep.
Then I lift my head, and brighten up,
It can't be this bad next week

ABOUT THE AUTHOR

Anthony Kitchen retired from a blacksmithing partnership in 2008. With the rise in popularity of open mic nights, he was then able to indulge himself in his bent for humorous satire, light-hearted poetry, doggerel, songs, and short stories.

Although his first efforts were in the early 1980s, it is only in later years he has been able to devote more time to writing. He trusts you will enjoy the humble efforts contained within.